I0091929

Narrative Productions of Meanings

Narrative Productions of Meanings

Exploring the Work of Stories in Social Life

Donileen R. Loseke

LEXINGTON BOOKS
Lanham • Boulder • New York • London

Published by Lexington Books
An imprint of The Rowman & Littlefield Publishing Group, Inc.
4501 Forbes Boulevard, Suite 200, Lanham, Maryland 20706
www.rowman.com

6 Tinworth Street, London SE11 5AL

Copyright © 2019 by The Rowman & Littlefield Publishing Group, Inc.

All rights reserved. No part of this book may be reproduced in any form or by any electronic or mechanical means, including information storage and retrieval systems, without written permission from the publisher, except by a reviewer who may quote passages in a review.

British Library Cataloguing in Publication Information Available

Library of Congress Cataloging-in-Publication Data

Names: Loseke, Donileen R., 1947- author.
Title: Narrative productions of meanings : exploring the work of stories in
    social life / by Donileen R. Loseke.
Description: Lanham, MD : Lexington Books, [2019] | Includes bibliographical
    references and index.
Identifiers: LCCN 2019001207 (print) | LCCN 2019013912 (ebook) | ISBN
    9781498577786 (electronic) | ISBN 9781498577779 (cloth)
Subjects: LCSH: Narrative inquiry (Research method) | Meaning (Psychology) |
    Social problems.
Classification: LCC H61.295 (ebook) | LCC H61.295 L67 2019 (print) | DDC
    300.72/3--dc23
LC record available at https://lccn.loc.gov/2019001207

Contents

Chapter One

Narrative and Productions of Meaning

From the beginning of life onward, people are drawn to stories, the common term for what academics call narratives. The promise of bedtime stories persuades toddlers into bed, young children watch Disney movies endlessly. While taste for particular kinds of stories often changes over time both for individuals and for societies, the appeal of stories does not. It is not surprising that stories are everywhere. They are the stuff of conversations with family and friends; they are in sermons, lectures, speeches, and testimonies in courts and policy hearings. Stories circulate endlessly on web pages, in media of all forms, on Twitter, and Facebook; they are the typical form of advertisements as well as what is analyzed by therapists. As noted by Roland Barthes (1977, 79), stories—narratives—are pervasive in social life in all times and in all places:

> Narrative is present in myth, legend, fable, tale, novella, epic, history, tragedy, drama, comedy, mime, painting . . . stained glass windows, cinema, comics, news, conversations. Moreover, under this almost infinite diversity of forms, narrative is present in every age, in every place, in every society. . . . Nowhere is nor has been a people without narrative. All classes, all human groups, have their narratives. . . . Narrative is international, transhistorical, transcultural: It is simply there, like life itself.

This book is about how stories produce meaning; about how this meaning can be a tool for sensemaking, persuading, and justifying; and about how narrative meaning-making shapes both subjective understandings and material realities on all stages of social life. I will start by laying out some basic characteristics of meaning and meaning-making in the current era which serves to place stories and storytelling within their contexts as well as outline why and how it is that narrative meaning-making is so important.

NARRATIVE AND MEANING

Jerome Bruner argues that the principle function of the human mind is "world making," forming meaning from the buzzing confusion of human experience (Bruner 1987, 11). Concern with questions about meaning is what unites a broad range of classical social theorists including philosopher Alfred Schutz, historian Max Weber, anthropologist Clifford Geertz, psychologist Sigmund Freud, and sociologists Peter Berger and Thomas Luckmann. Concern with meaning is shared by a variety of social theories including social constructionism, phenomenology, interactionism, and ethnomethodology. The following are some basic characteristics of meaning necessary to understand how narratives produce meaning and why this is important.

First, there are three types of meaning. Since the Enlightenment, academic observers of all varieties focus on examining *cognitive* meaning (Fisher 1984). While understanding what and how people think remains in the center of academic interest, scholars in a variety of disciplines now argue that emotion is a foundation of social life (for reviews, see Barbalet 2002; Marcus 2002; Moïsi 2009) and that social changes have led to the increasing tendency of people to worry less about what is thought and more about what is felt (McCarthy 2017). Hence, a second type of meaning is *emotional* (Loseke and Kusenbach 2008; McCarthy 2017; Moïsi 2009). Third, people are as much concerned about how the world should work as about how the world does work (Keen 2015; Pizarro 2000; Schwartz 2000); decisions are made based as much on evaluations of what is right as on what is practical or expedient (Fisher 1984; Jaspar 1992). This third kind of meaning, *moral*, is particularly important in an era characterized by dissention and disagreements. In short, understanding the power and importance of narrative meaning making requires appreciating how meaning is cognitive *and* emotional *and* moral.

Second, meaning has cultural, interactional, and personal dimensions. Chapter 2 explores how meaning is *cultural* because social orders contain circulating systems of meaning that can be components of a "cultural tool kit" (Swidler 1986) available for social actors to use as "schemes of interpretation" (Schutz 1970), "interpretive structures" (Miller and Holstein 1989), or "membership categorization devices" (Sacks 1972) which are general guidelines for how to think, feel, and act toward known and unknown people, objects, experiences, and events. On a case by case basis, people can choose to use, ignore, or modify their understandings of socially circulating meanings in order to "comprehend and organize experience" (Quinn 2005, 3; Gubrium and Holstein 1997, especially chapter 3).

Meaning also can be an *interactional* accomplishment. When systems of ideas are relatively shared, intersubjectivity is possible; intersubjectivity is the basis for interaction, interaction creates meaning. People therefore produce meaning in interactions. Finally, meaning is *personal* because, whether formed through face-to-face interaction, mediated through technologies, or located in texts, the unique experiences, agendas, and life circumstances of individuals influence what meaning is meaningful (Polkinghorne 1991). In short, meaning is cognitive, emotional, and moral; meaning can have cultural, interactional, and personal dimensions.

The final characteristic of meaning necessary to understand the importance of stories is, whether viewed through the lens of culture, interaction, or psychology, characteristics of the current era encourage a multitude of personal, social, and political problems surrounding meaning (see, for example, Alexander 2017; Calhoun 1994; Madsen et al. 2002; McCarthy 2017).

Some characteristics of this era encouraging problems with meaning are long-term social trends. Because what meaning is evaluated as meaningful depends upon individual characteristics, experiences, and life chances, increasing *heterogeneity* yields a population with very different understandings the world. Further, *population concentrations* (urbanization), leads to living among many strangers who routinely challenge individual understandings about how the world works and about how the world should work. And, *complexity* (from technology and globalization) creates environments defying easy comprehension, while rapid *change* leads to constant needs to revise understandings of the meanings of people, objects, events, experiences.

Other characteristics leading to troubled meaning are of more recent origin. For one, globalization, size, and complexity combine to produce no choice but to rely on media for facts about the world outside practical experience as well as for the meanings of these facts. Yet media is fragmented and offers multiple, often deeply conflicting visions of these facts and their meanings. Further, social media filters information in ways producing population segments who have very different knowledge about the world which influences what seems important or believable. Still further, a never-ending series of scandals—some real, some imagined—in government, religion, education, and media, have encouraged a loss of faith in institutions and institutional authorities making it not possible to know who or what can be trusted to produce meaning that can be trusted. Still further, politicians, pundits, and trolls knowingly and maliciously create meaning that is non-factual in non-random ways. Add to that the tendency for untruth to spread faster than truth because untruth typically is more interesting.

While there are countless other conditions exacerbating the problems of meaning in the current era, there is no need to belabor the point. In Ann Swidler's terms (1986), meaning is "unsettled." There are few objects, events, experiences, or people whose meaning is agreed upon by all, most, or even a majority of social members. What is evaluated as right and just and fair to some people is just as wrong and unjust and unfair to others. The shared meanings necessary for individual well-being, communication, and democratic governance are not necessarily present.

One question posed in such an era of troubled meaning is: What draws practical actors toward some systems of meaning rather than to others? The answer to this question about the current era has an ancient answer: People are drawn to meaning that appeals to thinking *and* to feeling *and* to moral evaluation (Aristotle 1926, 13–14). Such age-old reflections are confirmed by current observers who argue "cognitive beliefs about how the world is, our moral vision of how the world should be, and our emotional attachment to that world march in close step" (Jasper 1997, 108). This is what leads to the pervasiveness of narrative in all times and in all places.

Stories are a form of meaning-making that can simultaneously create all types of meaning: Stories can create *cognitive* meanings when plots transform what otherwise might seem isolated events into patterns; they can create *emotional* meanings when plots and characters encourage feelings; they can create *moral* meanings when characters and events encourage reflections on what is right or wrong. Stated otherwise, research and statistics appeal primarily to cognition; poetry, dance, and other artistic expressions appeal to emotion; religious texts appeal primarily to morality. The story form has the ability to appeal simultaneously to cognition, emotion, and morality. Taking seriously narrative potential to appeal to feeling is more common than in the past, but still not in the mainstream of social science disciplines tending to value (and therefore study) cognition and devalue (and therefore ignore) emotion (Harré 1986; Lutz 1986). Taking seriously narrative potential to speak to issues of moral concern likewise differs from academic tendencies to focus on seemingly objective "material interests" rather than seemingly subjective "moral values" (Hitlin and Vaisey 2013; Swidler 1986).

Stories create meaning. What this book is about is how the meanings made by stories do work in personal and social life. Most obviously, *meaning-making* itself is crucially important in a world where meaning is not fixed, agreed upon, or institutionally supported. The meanings made by stories, for example, are critical in building and maintaining an adequate sense of self and in offering guidelines for how to think and feel about, and act toward strangers in private life (chapter 3). The meanings produced by stories also can do the work of *persuasion*. Social activists and politicians alike know that stories about harms are far more effective than recitations of "facts" in persuading audiences that a condition must be changed because it is intolerable (chapter 4). The meanings produced by stories also can do the work of *justification*: Stories justify why people are accorded particular levels of moral worth, why public concern and resources should be spent in particular ways, why social policy, court rulings, or social services should be shaped in one way rather than another (chapter 5). Stories do work at all levels of social life; stories are political tools (chapter 6).

PRELIMINARIES FOR EXAMINING NARRATIVE PRODUCTIONS OF MEANING

As the philosopher, Alistar MacIntyre (1984, 216) stated so simply, "humans are a storytelling animal." All people know what a story is, how to recognize one, how to tell one; the story form is so common that it can seem the "impulse to narrate is natural" (White 1980, 5). Although we live in a world saturated with stories, rarely do we consider characteristics of the communication form; rarely do we ponder why some stories are told and retold while others are ignored or quickly forgotten. Although often assumed to be innocent conveyers of information, stories are a critical meaning-making resource, they are the scaffolding of social structure which produces and maintains injustices and inequalities of all types. Because I will argue throughout this book that seemingly obvious characteristics of stories can have critically important implications for how they can be used and for what they can do, I will begin with explicitly defining foundational ideas.

Narrative Content

There is remarkable variation in stories which can be as short as a sentence, as long as a multivolume novel or a television series that continues for many years. Stories can be told as fiction or fact, in poetry or prose; they can be sung, acted, danced, drawn, written, or spoken. Beyond these and many other differences, however, is a particular *content*. Although individual stories differ in the extent to which they attend to each of the following, stories typically contain scenes, events, and characters; each story is told for a reason and this is the story moral.

Stories are located in *scenes*, the particular settings in which story events unfold. Some stories, such as those about hurricanes, floods, famines, or war, are scene driven. Yet even if it remains in the story background, scene almost always is critical because story *meanings* are scene dependent: The meanings of story events and characters likely will differ depending on whether the story is set in 1818 or 2018, in New York City or Kabul.

Stories contain *events*, and these have four characteristics. First, with the exception of mysteries which contain a haphazard assortment of events meant to confuse, stories contain primarily those events needed to create the story. Second, story events are coordinated by a plot which links events into a coherent whole. In more formal terms, plot is a "structure of relationships by which the events contained in the account are endowed with a meaning by being identified as parts of an integrated whole" (White 1980, 13). Third, while story events do not need to be told in a linear fashion, events in a completed story have a time relationship to one another, which gives stories their potential to convey images of causality. Fourth, events achieve meaning by their contextualization within the story: A mundane event such as a "woman putting on makeup" can have vastly different meanings depending upon whether that event is located in a story about prostitution, about an abused woman attempting to hide her injuries, or about a happy bride preparing for her wedding.

Most stories contain *characters*. While these might be non-human (zombies, cartoon creatures, animals, cyborgs), the most important stories in social life feature human characters. At times, these characters are unique, named people; at other times stories contain categorical characters such as the "unemployed coal miner," or the "immigrant."

Finally, stories are told for reasons and these are story *morals*. Many categories of people—parents, preachers, teachers—tell stories specifically to convey moral lessons as do politicians who tell stories demonstrating the morality of voting one way or the other. Stories told in the course of daily life often are mundane reminders of obligations: A story about a friendship threatened by forgetting a birthday conveys the morality of remembering aspects of others' lives; stories about cars that do not start are morality tales about the importance of car maintenance or the benefits of new cars.

In sum, despite many variations, stories are recognizable because of story contents: Somewhere (scene) something happens (events) to someone/something (characters) and this conveys a lesson about something (moral). Although admittedly very brief, this description is sufficient to distinguish stories from other ways of presenting information which can be called the "non-story form." While non-stories can contain events and/or characters and/or scenes, what is distinctive about the story form is that it *contextualizes events which gives them meaning*. This distinguishes story from lists, bullet points, charts, chronologies, graphs, and statistics.

Sites of Narrative Production

Stories are produced on all stages of social life: Individuals produce *self-stories* (chapter 3); *organizations* produce stories about their work and clients (chapters 4 and 5); *institutions* produce stories about types of people requiring particular types of interventions (chapter 5). Some stories are known only to their authors or to relatively small groups of family or co-workers, other stories circulate widely so are well known.

While stories are created in different sites, there are reflexive relationships among stories produced on all stages of social life. For example, individuals might use their understandings of socially circulating stories to craft their self-stories; particular self-stories can become emblematic of types of stories; organizational workers use their images of a type of character, the client, in interacting with real clients; stories successful in social advocacy can become embedded in institutional responses to problems, and so on.

Narrative Authors and Audiences

Stories require two categories of people: Those who make stories (authors), and those who encounter and evaluate them (audiences).

As obviously follows from the previous section, stories are authored by individuals in daily life as well as by myriad categories of actors such as organizational workers and administrators, social movement activists, politicians, social policy makers, media personnel, and so on. That said, the authorship of stories can be complex. For example, some stories, such as that of the "American dream," were authored in the past and are continually challenged and modified over time (Rowland and Jones 2007). In such cases, original story authorship might not be as important as understanding the ways in which the story has changed over time and with what consequences. At other times, stories have multiple authors who are not actively collaborating to tell a story and who might be telling seemingly similar stories for very different purposes. For example, the "drowsy person" who is the main character in stories about accidents of many types has been produced through the distinctly not coordinated work of the National Sleep Foundation, auto insurance companies, sleep researchers, and mattress firms (Kroll-Smith 2000). In the same way, stories of ethnic identities have been co-authored by researchers, professional heritage preservers, ethnic leaders, ethnic organizations, and media (Berbrier 2000). To add more complexity, authorship of socially circulating stories can be unknowable or disguised; stories can be repeatedly modified as they "shared" or "retweeted," so a story as encountered might be far different from the story as originally written.

Stories also require *audiences*, the people who hear, read, or watch the story and who evaluate its worth. Authors write stories with particular audiences in mind. These audiences might be the self (internal conversations), particular people (family or friends), specific categories of people (such as audiences of voters or readers of the *New York Times*) or generic (the American public). What is notable about audiences in the current era is they are heterogeneous and fragmented which means any story likely will receive multiple—and often conflicting—interpretations.

Narrative Evaluation

Most stories told in private lives are inconsequential in that they are about mundane events told once or twice to family or friends (Linde 2010). What distinguishes such stories from those that go on to do important work in private and public lives? I will define a "good" story as one with the *potential* of being retold multiple times to relatively large audiences.

Most obviously, stories with such potential are evaluated as both *interesting* and *important* for the simple reason that stories regarded as boring or unimportant will be ignored. While there are remarkable variations in what is—and what is not—evaluated as interesting by individuals, there is less variation in the characteristics of stories deemed interesting by relatively large audiences. It is well known, for example, that people are drawn to stories containing characters or events that seem odd or unexpected rather than to those featuring unremarkable people or routine events; stories about events considered immediate and consequential are both more interesting and more important than those about events that seem distant or not consequential. Criteria for being evaluated as "interesting" also has changed over time because media tendencies to privilege stories characterized by drama and flash have led many people to become desensitized to all but stories containing the most extreme—if not downright bizarre—plots and characters (see Loseke 2003 for a review).

A story reaching the threshold of interest and importance has potential to be retold when it is evaluated as *believable*. Story believably, in turn, is judged through comparing perceived story contents with practical experience, commonsense, and judgments of morality. As Davis (2002, 17–18) says: "A good story is one that makes sense given what audiences think they know, what they value, what they regard as appropriate and promising." This leads to three important characteristics of story believability.

First, while my interest is in evaluations of perceived story *contents*, that is only one of multiple criteria by which stories are evaluated. There are stories—the focus of this book—and there is storytelling, the social interactions involved in the *performance* of communicating stories by specific people at specific times, in specific places, for specific purposes and so on (Alexander 2017; Alexander and Mast 2006; Polletta et al. 2011). I will return to the topic of storytelling in chapter 2. For now, the point is that while my interest here centers on questions about story contents, this is one of multiple factors influencing how particular stories are evaluated.

Second, believability is about comparing perceived story contents with personal experience and, the greater the heterogeneity, the greater the difference in experiences. Believability also is about evaluating the morality of perceived story contents and the current era is one of moral fragmentation where what is evaluated as obviously good and fair and just by some audiences is just as obviously bad and unfair and unjust to others. So, it should be expected that *very* few stories are judged as believable by the majority of people in a large, heterogeneous population and that most stories are judged as believable by some people and as not believable by others.

Third, a story is evaluated as *true* to the extent that it is believable with believability measured by the extent to which the story conforms to practical experiences, commonsense, and moral evaluations. Hence, story truth is experiential, moral, and emotional and there is *no* necessary relationship with "truth" as objectively measured or as grounded in expert opinion. A story having little relationship with the truth as objectively or scientifically measured nonetheless can be evaluated as true. I shall return to this in the final chapter.

NARRATIVE AND THE SOCIAL SCIENCES

Stories have been the object of philosophical attention throughout the ages. Plato, for instance, is said to have claimed that "those who tell the stories have the power," and Aristotle's thoughts on rhetoric continue to be foundational in literary techniques for examining stories (Frye 1957). Scholarly interest in stories also has a long history among literary critics interested in carefully crafted stories such as those in Greek myths, fairy tales, and the plays of Shakespeare as well as by scholars of religion attentive to the forms and meanings of stories in religious texts (Frye 1957; Polkinghorne 1991). Until the 1980s, however, social scientists tended to ignore stories because they were thought to be not important enough to warrant scholarly attention. Understanding why stories previously were ignored sets the stage for appreciating how and why they now are topics of interest throughout the academic social sciences (including anthropology, sociology, communications, criminology, women and gender studies, political science, and psychology) as well as professions such as education, law, medicine, and social work.

Social Science and the Natural Science Paradigm

When the social science disciplines started in the 1800s, they tended to adopt a "rational world paradigm" (Fisher 1984) which assumes humans are essentially rational, conduct is rule-bound, and the world is a set of puzzles awaiting scientific solution. Given such an orientation, the most acceptable research was modeled from the natural sciences with goals to discover general laws, the values of objectivity, and statistics as the preferred form of data (see Crotty 2015; Moses and Knutsen 2012 for elaboration). In multiple ways, questions about stories lie outside such frameworks: While concern within natural science paradigms is with understanding the *objective* world by *reducing* complexity, stories are about *subjective* meaning and *emphasize* complexity; while truth in the natural science paradigm is *objective* and *measurable*, story truth is *experiential, emotional,* and *moral*.

Although early Sociologists had attended to questions of subjectivity and values, efforts to gain credibility as a "science" in the mid-twentieth century led to attempts to unify the discipline around questions about objective reality (Rawls 2018), which led to devaluing interest in subjectivity, now deemed the "soft, subjective features of social life" (Hitlin and Vaisey 2013, 53). As summarized by Patricia Ewick and Susan Silbey (1995, 197–198):

> Scorned by scholars aspiring to scientific authority, narrative analysis was
> largely abandoned by social scientists in the 1930s and 1940s. Narratives were
> thought to be an ambiguous, particularistic, idiosyncratic, and imprecise way
> of representing the world.

One obvious antecedent to the 1980s social science discovery of narrative
was the increasing dissatisfaction with, and criticisms of, this natural science
framework (Calhoun and VanAntwerpen 2007; Steinmetz 2005). This included criticisms that the so-called "objectivity" of science disguised its
underlying complicity in supporting inequalities, as well as the inabilities of
this framework to answer questions posed by environments rapidly changing
from globalization, mass migrations, urbanization, and technology. Additionally, in the world outside academia, too much information radiating from too
many sources containing too many conflicting "facts" were serving to rela-
tivize truth. Replacing the previous importance of truth was emotion consciousness (McCarthy 2017). All of this change led then dominant social
science theories and research to be simply incapable of addressing important
questions and hence encouraged moving away from theoretical and methodological frameworks aligned with the natural sciences and toward frameworks
associated with the humanities. Constructionist philosophies of science, developed as an explicit opposition to natural science frameworks (Moses and
Knutsen 2012), offered ways to bring to the forefront questions of meaning
which opened possibilities for asking new questions and exploring them in
new ways.

The Narrative Turn

What is called the "narrative turn" in the social sciences was the moving
away from natural science models toward constructionist models, from examining questions of cause to questions of meaning, from conceptualizing
people as made by society to conceptualizing society as made by people.
Maggie Kirkman (2002, 30) describes how this changes conceptualizations
of research:

> Such changes are from a discipline concerned with measurement and predic-
> tion to one interested in description and understanding; from frequency and
> causation to meaning; from statistical analysis to interpretation; from numbers
> to language and symbols; from universals to particulars; from averages to
> individuals; and from attempting to decontextualise people and events to the
> study of people in their cultural context.

While natural science models value logic over emotion, facts over values,
objective description over subjective meaning, and specificity over contextualization, constructionist frameworks emphasize the importance of contextu-

alization and *question* distinctions between fact and value, objectivity and subjectivity, logic and emotion (Burr 2015; Crotty 2015; Moses and Knutsen 2012). This constructionist framework makes it legitimate to theoretically and empirically explore questions about meanings, feelings, and moralities (Denzin and Lincoln 2000; Ewick and Silbey 1995). Because narrative is a powerful tool of meaning-making, scholars cannot simply dismiss stories.

In brief, dissatisfaction with the natural science framework, coupled with changes in the social world created a *theoretical* need for social scientists to understand how people make meanings and how meanings make people. The need to understand meaning-making processes also is a matter of *practical* importance in a world increasingly characterized by disagreements so profound that debate and dialogue can seem not possible. Because the most common meaning-making tool is narrative, it follows that studies of meaning-making must take the work of stories seriously (see Denzin and Lincoln 2000; Berger and Quinney 2005).

Literary and Social Science Examinations of Narrative

Several important changes in how stories are conceptualized and studied are associated with moving stories from libraries to social life, and from the domain of literary criticism, film studies, and religious studies to the realm of social sciences. First, social scientists both changed and enlarged images of *what* stories are important to examine. Rather than explore characteristics of *fiction* of interest to literary critics, and *myth* of interest to religious scholars, social scientists typically are interested in stories told as *true*—regardless of the extent to which such stories conform to a truth as measured scientifically. Also, in comparison to literary critics who explore stories that are exceptionally well written and in final form, stories of interest to social scientists often are poorly written and in a constant process of revision. And, in comparison to literary critics who find their stories in libraries or other preservation sites, stories of interest to social observers are found in places such as court proceedings (Ewick and Silbey 1995; Nolan 2002), public policy hearings (Asen 2003; Stein 2001); newspapers (Clawson and Trice 2000); television (Barnett 2005); social advocacy documents (Berbrier 1998); political speeches (Coles 2002; Johnson 2002), and talk in support groups (Irvine 1999).

Social researchers also have expanded the notion of narrative genres from traditional sorts (comedy, tragedy, drama) to others such as the fictional genre of romance novels (Radway 1984), as well as nonfictional genres of autobiographies (M. Gergen 1994), social problems advocacy (Loseke 2003), and daytime talk shows (Squire 2002). Social scientists also changed images of what is important to examine. In comparison to literary critics who often are interested in the formal, structural properties of stories, social scientists tend to be more concerned with how stories are told, how they are used, and what work they perform in social life. As defined by Ken Plummer (1995, 19):

> a sociology of stories should be less concerned with analyzing the formal structures of stories or narratives as literary theory might, and more interested in inspecting the social role of stories, the ways they are produced, the ways they are read, the work they perform in the wider social order, how they change, and their role in the political process.

Finally, and critically, stories make meaning and this meaning does work in both private and public life. Understanding how stories work and the work stories do is a project with considerable *academic* potential. Further, because the meaning-making work of stories has very practical consequences, these explorations also are *practical* and *political*. In consequence, narrative exploration in the social sciences is a far more *politicized* endeavor than is typical in the study of works of fiction.

THEMES IN THE STUDY OF NARRATIVE PRODUCTIONS OF MEANING

My interest is located within a constructionist philosophy centered on questions about meaning production (Burr 2015; Crotty, 2015; Moses and Knutsen 2012). Four themes guide this exploration.

Narratives are Social in their Contents, Meanings, Evaluations, and Consequences

Everything about narrative is social. Stories are social in their *contents* because, in order for a story to be evaluated as believable, it must more-or-less reflect audiences' understandings of the typical meanings of objects, events, and people: Stories about "being possessed by the devil" are evaluated by most Americans in the current era as probably not true; stories of "mental illness" would not have been understandable to citizens of colonial America. The likely *meanings* of particular plots and characters depend upon audience evaluations, and these depend upon social environments. Likewise, stories are social in their *evaluations*. What probably is—and probably is not— evaluated as an interesting, important, and believable story depends upon audience members who bring with them their practical experiences as well as their understandings of how the world works and of how the world should work. Stories are social in their *consequences* because the work they do in sensemaking, persuading, and justifying leads to myriad consequences for individuals, organizations, institutions, and culture. Everything about narrative is social.

Narrative Meaning is Cognitive, Emotional, and Moral

A primary reason for the pervasiveness of stories in both private and public lives is that narrative meaning is cognitive, emotional, and moral. In various degrees and in assorted ways, stories can appeal to thinking, feeling, and morality. This is an important theme in a mass-mediated world where heterogeneity, a loss of belief in institutions and authority, and so on have increased the importance of emotional and moral truths while decreasing the importance of cognitive truth.

Narrative Meaning has Cultural, Interactional, and Personal Dimensions

A second primary reason for the pervasiveness of stories in both public and private lives is that the productions, consumptions, or consequences of narrative meaning are not confined to any particular realm of social life. Narrative meaning is about culture, it is about interactions, it is about psychology.

Narrative is a Tool of Power

In popular understandings, stories are fictional and fanciful, they are assumed to be trivial in their uses and insignificant in their consequences. In stark contrast, *regardless of any relationship to a scientific truth as established by research or experts*, stories are a tool of power. When appropriated as identity models, story characters locate individuals in social and moral hierarchies with accompanying constellations of rights, obligations, and opportunities. Stories can encourage publics to evaluate some—and only some—conditions as intolerable and in need of change, to accept some—and only some— policies and procedures as necessary and fair. Stories can become social structure through the institutionalization process (Alexander and Smith 1993), they can become models organizing action (Lamont and Fournier 1992). Stories are not innocent conveyers of meaning.

* * *

Chapter 2 examines relationships between narrative and culture, including cultural conventions surrounding storytelling as well as cultural meaning systems embedded in stories. Chapter 3 turns to questions about narrative and identity in private life and explores how story characters in general and the story characters of victim, villain, and hero in particular can be used as models of identity in making sense of self and others and how these influence evaluations of self and others in daily life. Chapter 4 moves to the world of social problems to consider how stories can be tools of persuasion convincing publics to evaluate particular conditions as morally intolerable and in need of change. Chapter 5 continues the theme of social problems and examines the multiple kinds of justifications stories provide in social policymaking and social service provision. Chapter 6 summarizes the personal, social, and political work of stories in the current era and concludes with practical implications of narrative productions of meaning for the political process in a world of troubled meaning.

Chapter Two

Narrative and Culture

In a world characterized by extraordinary differences in individual character-istics, experiences, opportunities, and world views, how is it possible for any specific story to be evaluated as interesting, believable, and important by more than a few people? My central arguments will be that stories cannot be understood outside of the cultures in which they are authored, told, and evaluated and that good stories are those incorporating cultural ways of thinking and feeling. This is about the cultural foundations of stories and storytelling (Bruner 1987; Gergen and Gergen 1983), and about how the meaning-making abilities of the narrative form come from how stories incor-porate socially circulating systems of meanings.

CULTURE

Constructionist philosophy leading to questions about how people make meaning and how meaning makes people necessarily leads to questions about culture. While there are multiple definitions of culture, as well as little agree-ment about how it should be analyzed (see, for example, Eberle 2009; Gans 2012; Lamont 2000b; Patterson 2004), I will draw from Clifford Geertz (1973, 5) who defines culture as well as the purpose of its analysis:

> Believing, with Max Weber, that man is an animal suspended in webs of significance he himself has spun, I take culture to be those webs, and the analysis of it to be therefore not an experimental science in search of law but an interpretive one in search of meaning.

Within this view, culture can be conceptualized as "publicly available sym-bolic forms" (Swidler 1986, 273), as circulating systems of ideas. Stories exist within specific cultures which provide both *systems of meaning* that can be used in authoring and evaluating stories as well as *guidelines* for story making, storytelling, and story evaluating. These guidelines and meanings are resources useful to story authors and story evaluators (Atkinson and Delamont 2006). Culture, then, can be understood as a tool kit (Swidler 1986), a "collection of stuff" (DiMaggio 1997) available for people to use as resources to accomplish practical agendas.

Two characteristics of culture define limitations of using it as an explanatory concept. First, just as heterogeneity among *people* is a defining characteristic of the current era, there is considerable heterogeneity in the perceived contents of culture so events, objects, experiences, and people can be understood quite differently by various audience segments that might be understood as "thought communities" (Zerubavel 1996). In consequence, the more heterogeneous the audience, the more likely story events, characters, and morals are evaluated in multiple ways; the more heterogeneous the audience, the more difficult it is to achieve agreement in evaluations of story interest, importance, and believability. Simply stated, culture in this era is fragmented.

Second, culture is a macro-level concept that can neither explain nor predict individual thoughts, feelings, or actions. So, although I will argue that cultural guidelines and meanings are both *resources* and *constraints* for story authors and evaluators, I will follow the stance of ethnomethodology (Heritage 1984; Weinberg 2008) and assume that practical actors decide to use, ignore, or creatively transform their cultural understandings on a case-by-case basis. Culture is not deterministic.

While culture is neither deterministic nor wholistic, communication nonetheless depends upon relatively shared meanings. Without shared meanings, stories could not be understood by other than their authors. Before moving to how culture shapes meanings in stories, I will start with how culture shapes the processes of storytelling.

CULTURE, STORYTELLING, AND STORYTELLERS

Storytelling is surrounded by expectations about where, when, and by whom what kinds of stories must be told, can be told and cannot be told, as well as about how story believability should be judged (Ewick and Silbey 1995; Linde 2010; Polletta et al. 2011).

Storytelling and Power

Cultural conventions embed storytelling within hierarchies reflecting and perpetuating *power*. Consider, for example, the many cultural conventions surrounding who has the right to request stories and who has the obligation to tell stories when requested. Specific categories of people (such as parents, social service providers, physicians, police) have the right to ask other categories of people (children, clients, patients, citizens) to tell stories, while these others have the obligation to tell the story requested. The right to request (or demand) stories reflects and displays power; the requirement to tell stories reflects and displays powerlessness.

Power also is manifested in what Amy Shuman (2005) calls *entitlement*: Who has the right to tell whose story? Some categories of people, such as children, those labelled mentally ill, and those deemed suffering from dementia, often are not entitled to tell their own stories. Their stories typically are told by others such as parents, teachers, counselors, and social workers who have the power to tell the stories of others, as well as the power to challenge contents and meanings of stories told by those not allowed to tell their own stories. Still other categories of people, such as journalists and ethnographers, regularly encounter the stories of others and package them in ways producing the particular kinds of meaning desired by those with the power to tell the stories of others.

Power also is visible in conventions surrounding evaluations of story *believability*. Stories told by parents, service providers, and medical personnel are assumed more believable than those told by children, clients and patients; stories told by prisoners are assumed untruthful. Further, stories told by people in disadvantaged categories such as African-American women (Collins 1989; Etter-Lewis 1991) or survivors of rape, incest, and sexual assault (Alcoff and Gray 1993) often are ignored.

Power enmeshed in the storytelling process is not fixed. To take an obvious example, while in the not-so-distant past, the believability of stories told by "scientists" was all but unquestionable, the current anti-science era challenges that power. In the same way, a series of scandals—some real, some imagined—in government, religion, and media have greatly reduced what had been somewhat automatic evaluations of the believability of stories told by officials in these institutions. Conversely, although women's stories of sexual harassment traditionally were either silenced or not believed, the #Metoo movement seeks to reverse that so that women's stories necessarily *will* be evaluated as believable.

Storytelling in Organizations

Another cultural convention surrounding storytelling is that *how* stories are told depends upon *where* and to *whom* stories are told. Practical actors know that stories told to friends can be remarkably different from those told to employers, that when a physician asks, "How are you?," the request is for a story centering on health, that when a lawyer asks a witness, "Tell me what happened," the request is for a story centering on the specific case being tried, and so on.

Of particular interest are conventions surrounding stories requested and told within organizations where guidelines can include where stories should begin, what events and characters stories should contain, and what morals they should emphasize (Holstein and Gubrium 2000; Linde 2009). Such guidelines can be formalized in social service intake forms and police crime reports that each request highly specific information combining to create the particular kind of story required by the organization (Eakin 2007).

Not surprisingly, organizational and client expectations about the preferred contents of stories can be remarkably different. Consider, for example, the case of South Africa's Truth and Reconciliation Commission Hearings. These hearings were organized to offer black South Africans a public space to tell their stories of the brutalities of Apartheid in order to psychologically heal. Yet black South Africans understood these hearings as a legal setting for assessing blame and allocating punishment. Due to such differences in expectations about the kinds of stories to be told, hearings failed to meet the goals of either their organizers or those telling their stories (Andrews 2007).

Differences between the kinds of stories required in organizational settings and storytelling in daily life lead to general tendencies of organizational clients to tell stories not conforming to organizational requirements (Polletta et al. 2011). Women victims of stalking, for example, often want to demonstrate to judges that they are active in discouraging their stalkers, yet such stories deter judges from viewing these women as utterly helpless victims who require court intervention (Dunn 2002). Women victims of intimate violence also often want to tell court workers about the complexity of their lives and relationships, yet these complexities can convince workers that court intervention will not be productive (Emerson 1997). In the same way, while judges in small claims courts want stories conforming to the rule-oriented accounts preferred by the legal system, litigants tend to tell complex stories centered on relationships among people in the events being litigated (Conley and O'Barr 1990). Given such common differences between organizational and client expectations about the contents of stories to be told, it is not surprising that workers can explicitly teach clients how to tell the kind of story required by the organization (Emerson 1997; Gubrium and Holstein 2000). Likewise, it is common for support groups (such as for people dependent upon alcohol or drugs) to not allow new members to tell stories until they are familiar with the groups' expectations for how and what stories should be told (Irvine 2000) and for seasoned members to specifically coach new members about what kinds of stories to tell (Mason-Schrock 1996; Loseke 2001).

Stories in organizations demonstrate both the power of organizations and the power of stories. Organizational power sets the terms and conditions of storytelling. Simply stated, clients wanting organizational services must tell the kind of story required by the organization. Hence, people identifying themselves as trans who wish to access hormone therapy or other medical interventions must secure a letter from a certified psychologist or physician specifically diagnosing them with "gender dysphoria." According to Spencer Garrison (2018, 619):

> Gender dysphoria is typically diagnosed through a series of life-history interviews, wherein the patient recounts their childhood experience of gender and explains how physical transition will benefit them. Thus, for persons seeking medical transition, narrative consistency becomes a paramount concern: these respondents face significant pressure to ensure that their stories meet the provider's expectations, as stories judged as unconvincing often yield denial of care.

A much different example demonstrating the power of organizationally determined conditions for stories as well as the power of stories is found in the process of asylum seeking. In order to be successful, refugees seeking political asylum in the United States must prove they have a well-founded fear of persecution in their homeland. This requires telling a story evaluated as a "persecution narrative" by authorities of the Bureau of Citizenship and Immigration Services. An asylum request is granted when an immigration judge evaluates the *story* as containing the legally required content of political persecution, and when the *storyteller* is evaluated as displaying expectable emotions while telling the story (Bohmer and Shuman 2007; McKinnon 2009; Shuman and Bohmer 2004).

Untellable Stories

While some stories must be told, and told in particular ways, other stories *cannot* be told. Some stories are untellable because they are *unspeakable*, with plots containing such horror that those who experienced it cannot find words to express what happened to them (Harvey et al. 2000). Such stories also can be *undiscussable* which means that storytellers who can find words and who *do* want to tell their stories learn audiences do not want to encounter stories that are so horrifying. Holocaust survivors immigrating to the United States did not talk about their horrific experiences to those not sharing this experience (A. Stein 2009); survivors of the Hiroshima bombing did not speak of what happened to them (Simic 2003); Americans who liberated the Nazi death camps did not share their experiences with others (Lifton 1973).

Stories evaluated as *incomprehensible* also lead to untellability because they find no audience. In a not-so-distant past, stories of "date rape" or "sexual harassment" were untellable. Such stories did not find audiences because they were incomprehensible (Shuman 2005), they were incomprehensible because they did not reflect cultural systems of meaning. Changes in these systems of meaning led such stories to become comprehensible and therefore tellable.

In summary, storytelling is a social activity governed by cultural conventions. While these are fragmented, situated, and not deterministic, they nonetheless shape what stories can be told by whom and where as well as how the believability of stories likely will be evaluated.

STORY MAKING, STORY EVALUATING, AND CULTURAL MEANINGS

Culture shapes story contents through systems of meaning I will call *cultural codes* (Alexander and Smith 1993) yet which go by other names such as semiotic codes (Swidler 1995), interpretive codes (Cerulo 2000), ideological codes (Smith 1999) or cultural coherence systems (Linde 1993). These systems of meaning are an aspect of what Emile Durkheim (1961) called the collective conscious, what Eviatar Zerubavel (1996, 428) calls the "impersonal archipelagos of meaning . . . share[d] in common." These systems of meaning are *resources* in that they can be used as the raw materials for meaning-making; simultaneously, they are *constraints* in that they limit what kinds of meaning likely will be evaluated as believable.

Stories become understandable for other than their author by incorporating systems of meanings that are relatively shared. Consider the following sentence contained in an article titled "Those Kids Said WHAT?! 28 Hilarious Real-Life Teacher Stories."

> As I welcomed my first-grade students into the classroom, one little girl noticed my polka-dot blouse and paid me the ultimate first-grade compliment: "Oh, you look so beautiful—just like a clown." (Sanwicki, n.d.)

Evaluating this sentence as both "hilarious" and a "story" requires drawing from a range of understandings about teachers, clowns, polka-dots, first graders, attractiveness, and compliments. When combined, these multiple understandings make an otherwise meaningless sentence into an "hilarious story."

Symbolic Codes and Emotion Codes

There are two sub-categories of cultural codes: Those surrounding ways of thinking, and those surrounding ways of feeling.

Cultural systems organizing ways of thinking are *symbolic codes*, which are densely packed and interlocking systems of ideas about how the world works, how the world should work; of rights, responsibilities, and relationships among people. Such codes are both statements of fact (how the world *does* work, how people *do* interact) as well as of moralities (how the world *should* work, how people *should* interact). Social life can be conceptualized as a web of meanings such as those of democracy (Alexander and Smith 1993), American values (Hutcheson et al. 2004), the American way of life (Johnson 2002), violence (Cerulo 1998), good health (Edgley and Brissett 1990), and individualism (Bellah et al. 1985). Each such system of meaning can be resources to construct as well as to evaluate story plots and morals. Other systems of meaning such as citizen and enemy (Alexander 1992), citizen and terrorist (Flopp 2002), victim (Holstein and Miller 1990; Best 1997; Lamb 1999), villain (Brooks 1976; Loseke 2009; Singer 2001), and hero (Klapp 1954; Chang 2002; Rankin and Eagly 2008) can be used to construct as well as to evaluate story characters.

Cultural codes include *emotion codes*, also called emotionologies (Stearns and Stearns 1985), emotional cultures (Gordon 1990), and feeling rules, framing, rules, and display rules (Hochschild 1979). These are cognitive models about which emotions are expected when, where, and toward whom or what, as well as how emotions should be inwardly experienced, outwardly expressed, and morally evaluated (Loseke and Kusenbach 2008; Lutz 1986). As with symbolic codes, emotion codes contain both expectations of what is (how people *do* tend to feel and emotionally express themselves in specific situations, how particular emotions *are* morally evaluated) as well as what *should* be (how people *should* feel and emotionally express themselves, how particular emotions *should* be evaluated). Codes such as sympathy (Clark 1997), empathy (Ruiz-Junco 2017), compassion (Höijer 2004), jealousy (Stearns 1990); anger (Lambek and Solway 2001), love (Swidler 2001; Cancian 1987), fear (Altheide 2002), pity (Boltansi 1999), disgust (Hancock 2004), and closure to grief (Berns 2011) are the building blocks of stories encouraging or discouraging particular kinds of emotional response.

While distinct in theory, symbolic and emotion codes are inextricably connected in practice because thinking and feeling cannot be separated (Loseke and Kusenbach 2008; McCarthy 1989, 2017). "War" and "family" are as much felt about as thought about, victims and villains encourage particular ways of feeling as well as ways of thinking, and so on. Story content often is composed of interwoven threads of cognitive and emotional meaning; stories incorporating both symbolic and emotion codes can yield one of the primary powers of the narrative form which is the ability to appeal *simultaneously* to thinking and feeling.

Consider the following story, a segment from an "Oprah Life Class" titled "Bishop T.D. Jakes Gives Feuding Sisters a Reality Check" (September 27, 2013). This story incorporates multiple elements of a *cultural* code of family which includes elements of a *symbolic* code (what family is, the importance of family, how families do and should function, how family members do and should act toward one another) and an *emotion* code (the expectation and importance of love among family members, the meaning of anger among family members).

> Carrie and Casey are sisters who haven't spoken in six years because Carrie feels her sister betrayed her by emailing with her ex-boyfriend. Though Casey says it wasn't sexual, Carrie feels they crossed a line. . . . Bishop T.D. Jakes steps in to help these feuding siblings understand the importance of family. "You're speaking two different languages," Bishop Jakes tells Carrie and Casey. "Which happens in families all the time. Casey admits she made a mistake by talking to her sister's ex, but thinks Carrie has forgotten all of the good things she's done to help her in the past. "You're talking about what you did for her," Bishop Jakes says. "And you probably did do them. And you probably came through in a lot of ways and it's not about you not being a good person. . . . What they can all agree on is that Carrie and Casey still love each other, or they wouldn't be at "Lifeclass" asking for help. "You both love each other or you wouldn't be angry," Bishop Jakes says. "You don't get angry with people you don't care about. Your anger is a picture of your love." But by being angry, Bishop Jakes says they've lost sight of what's really important. "You're being robbed of the gift of a sister," Bishop Jakes says. "Do you know what you lose when you lose a sister? Somebody who really loves you and has got you and understands you. We let too many people come in and tear down our family relationships. You've got to get your family relationship together." Bishop Jakes says he doesn't think Casey meant to hurt her sister. "I think you're hurt that she's hurt and that you can't figure out how to get back," he says. Carrie interrupts. "She didn't accidentally try to date my boyfriend," she says. "It wasn't like it was an accident. "No," Bishop Jakes says. "It's not an accident. But it's not leukemia, either. "The audience applauds as Bishop Jakes puts the sister's argument into perspective. "You cannot make these things mountains because then when the mountain does come, you don't have the strength to climb," he says. "This is not a mountain. It is a misunderstanding. You can't afford to fall out with her. That's your sister. That's your sister. Look at her. That's your sister. She shares your blood, your DNA, your philosophy. She knows your history. That's your sister. She is worth the fight to get it back. She is worth the fight to get it back. Climb over whatever you've got to climb over and get each other back." (Oprah's Life Class 2013)

As elements of culture, the perceived *contents* and *importance* of any system of meaning are situated and understood in different ways by different audience segments. Given the fragmentation characterizing the current era, no particular content likely will lead a story to be evaluated as believable and important by all, or even most, practical actors. Yet one story, that of the American Dream, has maintained a remarkable power over time to be so evaluated by very large audiences in the United States.

An Illustration: The American Dream Story as Cultural Code

No story in the United States has been the object of as much social science attention as the story of the American Dream (such as Brands 2010; Cramer 2016; Cullen 2003; Gest 2016; A. Hochschild 2016; Lamont 2000a; Loseke 2018; Rowland and Jones 2007; Samuel 2012; Sherman 2009; Silva 2013; Vance 2016). For several reasons, this story is particularly interesting.

First, while a characteristic of the current era is that stories often circulate in quite narrow population segments and receive very different evaluations from various segments, the American Dream is known by virtually all Americans and has been evaluated as important and believable by large audiences for almost 100 years. Indeed, observers argue this story is as central to liberal democracy as the Constitution (Rowland and Jones 2007). Lawrence Samuel (2012, 2) believes this story is "woven into the fabric of life" in the United States:

> Rather than just a powerful philosophy or ideology, the American Dream . . . is thoroughly woven into the fabric of everyday life. It plays a vital, active role in who we are, what we do, and why we do it. No other idea or mythology has as much influence on our individual and collective lives.

The Dream story also is interesting because its characters and plots can be read within either the themes of morality/community *or* materialism/individualism (Fisher 1973; Medhurst 2016; Rowland and Jones 2007). I will focus my comments on the materialist/individualist version for the practical reason that it is—by far—the most widely held and deeply embraced understanding of the story in this era. So much so that current commentators rarely even mention alternatives to the materialist/individualist version. While I will follow current conventions and label this the story of the American Dream, properly it should be called the "materialist/individualist version of the American Dream." I will return to this in chapter 6 and argue that those interested in social justice would do well to consider the potentials of the now-suppressed community/morality version of this story.

Additionally, the story in its currently popular form is interesting because it can be understood as the storied form of a set of widely held and deeply embraced cultural codes: Individualism (the values of self-determination and self-responsibility), capitalism (the values of work, private profit), fair play (the value of equality of opportunity) meritocracy (the value of rewards based on achievement), and family (the value of attachment to, and responsibility for a defined set of others).

Finally, the American Dream is particularly interesting because, while composed of cultural codes, the story itself is a cultural code defining visions of the world as well as preferred ways of acting, thinking, and feeling in that world. As such, the story is a cultural tool for making sense of self and others.

The American Dream is a *formula story* (Berger 1997) in that it contains characters, plots, and morals that are predictable. I will start with two examples of this formula story and use them to develop formula story characteristics.

The first example is from an article titled "10 People Living the American Dream" contained on a website," The Street," which offers investment advice:

> Chris Gardner's life story was dramatically retold in the Will Smith movie, The Pursuit of Happyness. Gardner was raised by a single mother but forced from his home as a young man as a result of her bad relationship with an abusive boyfriend. . . . Later Gardner joined the Navy and, working as a medical supply salesman, married and had a child. Fatefully, after seeing a well-dressed man in a sporty Ferrari, Gardner asked what he did for a living. The man, Bob Bridges, answered that he was a stockbroker and offered to help Gardner with interviews for training programs at some of New York's largest brokerage houses. He was accepted into a training program at E.F. Hutton, but his spate of bad luck returned quickly. The man who hired him was fired and the program was no longer open to him. Soon thereafter, he was arrested and had to spend a brief stint in jail for having amassed $1, 200 in parking tickets. He returned home to discover that his wife had left him. Gardner was able to earn a position in the training program at Dean Witter Reynolds, pass the licensing exam and be offered a position by Bear Stearns in San Francisco. But he was still destitute and homeless, forced to work the job by day and at night, after getting his son from day care, search for a hot meal and safe place to sleep. He later was admitted to a homeless shelter and, throughout the ordeal, never let on to his co-workers that his personal life was in such dire straits. Hard work eventually paid off. Gardner was able to finally provide for himself and his son and growing success led to the formation of his own firm, Gardner Rich & Co., in Chicago. (Started with a mere $10,000 in seed money, it was run out of his apartment.) The firm grew, was later sold in a multimillion-dollar deal, and Gardner went on to be CEO of a new venture, Christopher Gardner International Holdings. In talking about the man he learned to portray in The Pursuit of Happyness, Smith said it: "Chris represents the American Dream." (Lamonth, July 4, 2011)

The second example of the American Dream formula story is from an online version of *Success* magazine which offers "inspiration, motivation, and training for success in all areas of life." Told by an anonymous narrator, the story is titled "An Immigrant's Take on Today's American Dream":

> My parents and I arrived in the U.S. when I was 3 on an air-conditioned Greyhound bus with all of the proper documents in hand. When we reached our destination in downtown Dallas, we took a taxi from the bus terminal to my aunt's house. In one of my earliest memories, I recall feeling overwhelmed

with astonishment seeing the Dallas skyline for the first time. . . . America looked and felt like a dream. My mom tells a story of our first night in America: Before going to bed, I asked her if we could sleep with our eyes open. She asked me why I wanted to do that, and I told her I was afraid that if we closed our eyes and fell asleep, we would wake up back home in Mexico and realize that it was all a dream. She assured me it wasn't, and that America was our home now. It's now been our home for more than 20 years. Over that time, I've met plenty of other people who moved from Mexico, both legally and illegally. And plenty of people who've moved here from other parts of the world, too. With very few exceptions, what nearly every one of them has in common is the dream that if they work hard enough, they can improve their place in life and the lives of their children. I see this in Esperanza Gonzales, who emigrated from Mexico and built her restaurant inside a convenience store to pay for her daughter's college tuition . . . I see it in my barber Alberto, who cuts hair to support his son's tuition as well. . . . These stories, about a willingness to work for a better life even when conditions aren't always favorable, are uniquely American tales that everyone, regardless of politics, should celebrate. (Jimenez 2017)

The Contents of the Story of the American Dream

The American Dream is a formula story in that specific instances of the story, such as those of Chris Gardner and an anonymous immigrant, contain predictable constellations of settings, characters, plots, and morals.

Setting is critical to the American Dream story which, of course, takes place in the United States. While rarely explicitly stated, the story *invariably* assumes that this is a place of endless opportunities which allow frequent and widespread economic mobility. Chris Gardner, for example, found opportunities for employment in the stock market, the anonymous immigrant tells stories of other immigrants who found opportunities to open restaurants and barber shops. The American Dream is a rags to riches story, with riches made possible by the endless opportunities available within the scene of the United States.

Stories have characters and the American Dream is a *character-driven* story featuring what I will call the "good American" character distinguished by *behavior*, *motivation*, and *psychological disposition*. With a central goal of achieving self-reliance, this character engages in endless labor; problems are met with resolve and optimism; failures lead to harder work. As read through the cultural codes of individualism and capitalism, the good American is a distinctly *moral* character, dedicated to achieving self-reliance through individual effort. This character is not selfish because the American Dream also incorporates the code of family and motivations for *self*-reliance often center on what is good for *family*: Chris Gardner was heroic in caring for his son; Esperanza Gonzales built her restaurant "to pay for her daughter's college tuition;" Alberto, the barber, cuts hair to "support his son's tuition."

As important as what is assumed central in defining the good American character is what is excluded: This character has no particular gender, race, ethnicity, ability, sexuality, age, or religion. Indeed, the good American character is not even necessarily an American citizen—the restaurant owner Esperanza Gonzales and Alberto, the barber, are immigrants whose citizenship is not clear.

Stories take place in scenes and have characters. They also feature events liked into *plots*. The American Dream is a simple story featuring events of never-ending trials and tribulations, responded to with unceasing hard work. In ideal form, the story has a happy ending: Hard work and sacrifice pay off and success, as measured by money, social standing, and family well-being, is achieved. Gardner's success cannot be debated for, after all, his story was deemed worthy of transforming into a movie featuring a Hollywood star; new immigrants find that hard work can "improve their place in life and the lives of their children."

Finally, stories have morals and the moral of the American Dream is that success comes from *individual* behaviors, motivations, and attitudes. As told, Gardner's success was of his own making. Supports—he and his son lived in a homeless shelter, several people found him jobs—are in the background and the story remains tightly focused on his individual efforts. Audiences are encouraged to assume that individual effort alone can lead "illegal and legal" immigrants from "many countries" to open small businesses and earn sufficient money to send their children to college. As read within the codes of individualism and capitalism, the American Dream is a story with a moral that the world *does* work as it *should* work: Success comes to those who play by the rules of individualistic capitalism.

Because the American Dream is a formula story, individual instances of it can be recognized even when audiences are not explicitly told that a particular story is an instance of this type of story. The following story, "Oscar Winner Viola Davis Tells USF Crowd: 'Own Your Own Story,'" is *not* explicitly called a story of the American Dream yet it contains all the elements of the formula story. It is about a character born into a life of "abject poverty, racial and domestic abuse" who figured out who she "wanted to be" and then became that person and reached the pinnacle of success. As typical, the story of her route to success does not include anything seeable as "breaks" or "good luck;" it includes only her determination. Indeed, in this particular story the character seems to have simply willed her own success:

> Two-time Tony winner. Emmy honoree. Yet those aren't Davis' greatest accomplishments. Davis, 51, testified about a hard life before success, marred by abject poverty, racial and domestic abuse and various insecurities. Demons

that Davis compared to a scene in *The Exorcist*, when the words "help me" erupted on a possessed girl's skin. "That's how I see the journey of living one's authentic life," Davis said. "We're possessed by others' dreams. . . . But in there is a voice, a space in your body that lets you know exactly who you are. . . . My name is Viola. And I am a hero, but I don't have a cape. I don't have superpowers." Instead, Davis evoked the teachings of Joseph Campbell, a concept of the hero's quest from ordinary beginnings to extraordinary ends. . . . Much of Davis' presentation dealt with life long before fame. . . . A life lived in "abject poverty" in South Carolina with a drunken, abusive father, submissive mother and bigoted classmates. . . . Davis recalled being kept awake at night by the sound of pigeons eating rats infesting her home, and boys chasing her after school, hurling rocks and epithets. . . . Her revelation came while watching Cicely Tyson's landmark performance in the 1974 movie *The Autobiography of Miss Jane Pittman*. "I knew then what I would do," Davis said,"who I wanted to be." That sort of personal assertion was at the heart of her lecture: "Own your own story," she counseled. (Persall 2011)

The American Dream formula also is recognizable in "Undocumented & Unafraid: Anthony's Story." Despite a lack of citizenship—indeed, despite a lack of documentation—Anthony and his parents are examples of the good American character: His parents work tirelessly "to provide for our family's needs," Anthony has a "determination to succeed." The story has the preferred happy ending: Hard work paid off and Anthony obtained a college degree from a prestigious university.

In 2001, my Nanay (Mom in Tagalog) made the hardest decision of her life—leaving my two siblings and me behind in the Philippines in order to seek a better life and future for our family. While we came a few months later, my parents had to work long hours just to put food on the table and provide for our family's needs. . . . They worked tirelessly to prove that they made the right choice for our family to move to the U.S. . . . When I started to apply for college, I realized my life was limited by not having a social security number but I was determined to succeed no matter what. In 2011, I graduated from University of California- Irvine with a Bachelors of Art in Political Science. (United We Dream, n.d.)

The American Dream as Cultural Resource

While the story achieves its power by weaving together into story form several widely held and deeply embraced cultural codes in the United States, the American Dream story itself is a cultural code, a system of expectations about what is and about what should be. As such, the story can be used as a meaning-making resource.

The American Dream, for example, can be used as a model for how the world *should* work and for how people *should* act. Observers have documented how people in the American working class explicitly and routinely use their understandings of this story as a template for how the world should work and as a yardstick to evaluate morality. Within the world of the American dream, adults *should* work even when jobs are demeaning and the pay is low, they *should* take care of their family members, they *should* do so without complaint. Such morality, in turn, can be a model justifying *social and moral hierarchy*: Those who work and care for family should be accorded higher moral standing than those who do not (Cramer 2016; Gest 2016; A. Hochschild 2016; Lamont 2000a; Loseke 2017; Sherman 2009; Silva 2013, Vance 2016).

Because the story of the American Dream is "one of the precious few things in this country that we all share" (Samuels 2012, 2), it also can be used to encourage voters to support all varieties of political agendas. The following, for example, was an entry in the blog,"Florida Politics," about a political advertisement for a Republican running for state representative:

> Dover state Rep. Ross S. has started running his first TV ad in the race for Florida's 15th Congressional District, pitching himself as a candidate who will fight to keep the American Dream "alive and well." The ad, titled "American Dream," sees the Hillsborough County Republican touch on that concept before rattling off a litany of outside attacks against it. "My dad taught me that if you work hard, honor God and treat people right, you can succeed. That's our American Dream," S. says in the ad. Then a record scratch hits and the ad flashes between images of some of the most disliked politicians, pundits and groups among Republican circles. . . . "But now career politicians, special interests and liberals are working to kill that dream, attacking our rights and increasingly our values. I'll fight back for you in Congress, so the American Dream is alive and well for the next generation." (Wilson, 2018)

The story is just as effective in promoting those running as Democrats. In the following letter to the editor in the *Miami Herald*, the speaker uses his own credentials as a good American to promote a Democratic candidate as another good American:

> Gillum, as the son of a school bus driver and construction worker and the first in his family to graduate college, has much more in common with our story than DeSantis [the Republican candidate] ever will. In fact, his story is very similar to my own. Coming of age in the United States, I studied hard and worked every day after school. I joined the military. After my service I began a career as a door-to-door insurance salesman. Since then, I have started and acquired 27 companies. I have succeeded in America beyond my wildest dreams. These companies have created thousands of jobs, and I am proud to have contributed more than $100 million to benefit children's education and healthcare. As a successful businessman, I can tell you that Andrew Gillum is the better choice in the upcoming election. I support Gillum because his plans for affordable healthcare, a great education for every child, good-paying jobs and opportunity for everyone are the pillars of the American Dream. These are

what made my story possible and these are the things Gillum will fight for. (Fernandez 2018)

In the following chapters I will offer many more examples of the ways in which the story of the American Dream is more than a story that happens to be evaluated as important and believable by large audiences. The story does a great deal of meaning-making work, not all of which has positive consequences.

The American Dream story (more properly, the materialist/individualist version of the story) circulates widely on many stages of social life which indicates that significant numbers of Americans evaluate it as believable and important. Regardless, social observers are relentless in their condemnation of this story (Best 2018), criticizing it as an ideological disguise of the actual structure of opportunities in the United States which is criticized as racist, classist, sexist, homophobic, ageist, ableist, and xenophobic (for example, Frank 2004; J. Hochschild 2001; Jackson 2012; Porter 2010).

Additionally, in the preferred ending of this story, the good American character is richly rewarded for endless toil and perseverance. Social life, of course, produces countless examples of individuals whose motivations, attitudes, and behaviors are clearly those of the good American character who nonetheless do not achieve even a modicum of economic well-being for self or family. Meaning-making problems follow from failures of central cultural myths to make sense of practical experiences.

And, stories of any type offer only the most general of criteria for making sense of self, others, objects, and experiences. As such, the American Dream results in countless questions and problems in evaluating the extent to which particular people in particular situations align with story characters and plots: How do multidimensional, complex, and often seemingly contradictory characteristics of real people fit expectations of the story? How much can real people seemingly veer from the exemplar good American character before they are not this type of person? Who decides what constitutes an important divergence between the model and individual characteristics? As a cultural code, all the story can do is offer a general system of expectations. On a case-by-case basis practical actors must decide which people and which experiences are exemplars of the American Dream.

NARRATIVE AND CULTURE

While culture in the current era is fragmented and contested, cultural foundations of stories and storytelling nonetheless shape how, when, where, and by whom stories must be told, can be told, cannot be told as well as what kinds of story contents encourage particular audiences to evaluate a story as believable and important. Two topics deserve further discussion.

First, as elements of culture, there are wide variations in the extent to which symbolic and emotion codes are known and perceived to be important. "Wedding etiquette," and "freedom," for example, are two codes yet few would doubt that the code of freedom is far more widely known and centrally important in social life than the code of wedding etiquette. The kinds and extents of variations in how particular audiences evaluate particular stories are empirical questions, and variations have consequences for stories. Because the "most inherently powerful frames are those fully congruent with schemas habitually used by most members of society" (Entman 2003, 422), the more heterogeneous the population, the more likely stories receiving widespread approval will steer clear of contentious codes such as social class, religion, race/ethnicity, and sexuality (Loseke 2009). It is therefore predictable that the character of the "good American" in the American Dream story is without class, religion, race/ethnicity, and sexuality as such characteristics would reduce the perceived universal nature of the story.

Second, my rendition of culture began very idealistically with culture as systems of conventions and understandings informing storytelling, story content, and story evaluation. Yet there soon appeared glimpses of how these conventions and understandings can yield very real practical consequences: Only some people can tell their stories, only some stories can be told, stories can be used as guidelines for evaluating self and others, some stories—and only some stories—will lead to needed social resources, stories justify social hierarchies. While social observers often distinguish between culture and structure (see Gans 2012), between idealism and materialism, stories reflecting cultural understandings can go on to shape material realities.

Chapter Three

Narrative and Identity

The multiple problems of meaning in this era create identity as a common site of trouble: How is it possible to make sense of the self within constantly changing environments characterized by disagreements and contention? How is it possible to know how to think and feel about as well as how to act toward strangers? I will argue that stories—both those authored by the self as well as by others—are a primary meaning-making tool for answering questions about the identity of self and others in daily life.

IDENTITY AND ITS DILEMMAS

Identity is about self-classification (answers to "Who am I?" questions), classification of others ("Who are they?"), and about how others classify the self ("Who am I to them?"). Identity sorts unique individuals into an ever-increasing number of *social* categories such as those associated with social class, race/ethnicity, gender, sexuality, citizenship, family, religion, occupation, political identification, deviance, and so on.

Identity categories can be understood as *cultural codes*, densely packed systems of meaning about anticipated *appearances*, *personal characteristics*, and *behaviors* as well as expectations of *rights* and *obligations*. Identity codes also are *social and moral evaluations*. Regardless of the personal characteristics of individuals, those in some identity categories (such as veteran or nun) are accorded more esteem and higher moral worth than others (such as addict or thief). Social and moral evaluations, in turn, link identity categories with *emotion codes*: Categories accorded moral worth are associated with positive emotions (admiration or respect from those evaluating the category, pride for those in the category), while devalued or condemned categories are associated with negative emotions (disdain or even hostility from those evaluating the category, embarrassment or shame for those in the category). Finally, particular constellations of expectations and evaluations accompanying particular identity categories are associated with the presence or absence of various kinds and magnitudes of *social and economic opportunities*: Regardless of personal characteristics or abilities, those in the category of "Harvard law graduate" enjoy more opportunities than those in the category of "high school dropout."

Although identity is multiply consequential, characteristics of the current era lead to rapid change in expectations and evaluations associated with particular identity categories as well as little agreement about what these evaluations and expectations should be. Such complexity in meaning raises practical questions: How is it possible to have a stable understanding of the *self* when there are so many choices, so many disagreements, so much change? (Calhoun 1994; Holstein and Gubrium 2000; MacIntyre 1984; McAdams, 1996). The era also raises questions about the identities of *others*: Daily life in urban areas requires sharing space and interacting with a variety of others. Yet when these others are strangers, how is it possible to know what to expect, how to act, who can be trusted? Scholars from a variety of disciplines argue that a way—perhaps a primary way—in which such questions about identity are answered is through *story characters*.

PERSONAL AND CATEGORICAL IDENTITIES IN NARRATIVES

The stories most important for answering questions about identity contain human characters (as opposed to animals or cartoons) and plots more-or-less reflecting real-life events (as opposed to science fiction or fantasy). Human characters in such stories are of two types: unique embodied people and categorical people.

The most common story character is a unique, embodied *individual*. Consider the following excerpt from a newspaper article titled "Europeans in U.K. Gripped by Fear":

> A tsunami of uncertainty has engulfed Anna W., a Polish restaurant worker in London, since Britain voted to leave the European Union. Would her two teenage children, who grew up in the United Kingdom, still qualify for loans to study at British universities? Would she and her husband, after 11 years of working here, have to sell the home they just bought? The 41-year old is among the hundreds of thousands of EU workers in Britain who are fearful and confused over what happens next as their adoptive country begins the long process of unwinding its many ties to continental Europe. (*Tampa Bay Times* 2016)

The main character in this story is a particular woman, Anna W., who lives in London, is an employed restaurant worker, Polish, 41 years old, a married homeowner with two teen children. Cultural codes associated with individualism in the United States would encourage audiences to morally evaluate her as a responsible person because she is married, a mother, a homeowner, and employed for many years.

Such stories featuring unique characters are of *personal identities*. These stories have many authors and are a pervasive feature of social life. People regularly tell stories featuring themselves, friends, and family as primary characters; researchers and reporters, politicians and preachers commonly pepper their reports, speeches, sermons, and lectures with such stories. Stories featuring individual characters also are typical contents of magazines, blogs, television shows, and movies.

A second type of narrative character is a disembodied *category* of person. Such categorical characters are of identity as a social classification (DiMaggio 1997; Lamont and Fournier 1992) or collective representation (Durkheim 1961). Consider again the story, "Europeans in U.K. Gripped by Fear." While Anna W. is the primary character, the story also features a categorical character, the "EU worker in Britain." What audiences know about this category of person is that there are "hundreds of thousands" of them, they are from the European Union (they are not British citizens), they are responsible (they are "workers"), and they have particular emotions (they are "fearful and confused"). All that is important about categorical characters is what is related to their categorical identity: Victim categorical characters are known only as they are victims, heroes only as heroes, and so on. So, the name, age, family, unique experiences, and so on are not important for the "EU worker" whose part in the story is that of a good worker from the European Union who lives in Great Britain and is fearful and confused about the consequences of Brexit.

Narratives featuring categorical characters have a variety of authors: Presidents of the United States regularly tell stories about "Americans" (Coles 2002; Johnson 2002), television talk shows create narratives of cultural outsiders such as "sexual minorities" (Gamson 1998), "white trash" (Squire 2002), or "immoral sinners" (Lowney 1999); newspapers construct characters such as the "poor" (Clawson and Trice 2000), the "deserving poor" (Loseke and Fawcett 1995), or the "crack baby" (Lyons and Rittner 1998); and social movement activists create new categorical identities such as "gays and lesbians" (Bernstein 1997) and the "battered woman" (Rothenberg 2002).

Stories often contain a mix of unique and categorical characters. A common journalism practice is beginning an article about an event, such as a fire or a crime spree, with the story of a particular person or family affected by that fire or victimized in that crime spree. Politicians likewise tend to sprinkle stories of unique individuals in particular situations into their speeches about types of people in types of situations, just as social activists use stories of individual people experiencing hardship to exemplify a general problem; policy makers use stories of individuals to justify the need for policies targeted to categories of people, and so on. In all such instances, audiences are asked to assume a *unique* story character is an adequate representative of the *categorical* character. So, "Europeans in UK Gripped by Fear" implicitly asks audiences to assume that the story of one character, Anna W., exemplifies a type of character—the "hundreds of thousands" of people who are instances of the "EU worker in Britain." When such stories are used as meaning-making tools in public spheres, this relationship between a unique character and a categorical character is consequential because the stories of one or a few individuals can shape both public opinion and public policy for categories of people.

STOCK CHARACTER TYPES, CULTURAL MEANINGS, AND IDENTITIES

Some story characters are "stock" characters in that they are well known and common in a variety of stories told for assorted reasons in private and public life. One such stock character is the "good American," other stock characters include fools, do-gooders, city slickers/country hicks, average Joes, and so. The characters of *victim*, *villain*, and *hero* are particularly important because they are the "essential triad of protest, mobilization for war, and other instances of political oratory" (Bergstrand and Jasper 2018).

The Victim Character

While dictionaries define "victim" simply as a person who has been harmed, a victim designation in practice is more complex because victim is a symbolic code, an end result of a series of cognitive and moral appraisals that this is a *good* person, *greatly harmed*, through *no fault*, and for *no good reason* (Best 1997; Holstein and Miller 1990; Loseke 2003). Because the victim symbolic code is associated with the emotion code of sympathy, designating a person as a victim also requires an *emotional* appraisal: Victims are those evaluated as deserving the emotion of sympathy and its behavioral expression of help (Clark 1997).

The victim symbolic code can be used as a guideline for authoring a "perfect" victim character. The title of the following story, "Severe Neglect and Abuse as a Child Sent One Man on a Lifetime Journey of Healing," directs audiences to evaluate this as a story of great harm creating great injury. Notice how the story contains *nothing* that encourages—or even allows—evaluating the harm as created for a "good reason," or for evaluating the story character as responsible for creating the harm experienced. Christopher is a pure victim. As such, this story encourages the emotion of sympathy and evaluations that Christopher deserves the help he is receiving:

> Christopher grew up with domestic violence, but not the paradigm experience one might think of. "My father never laid a hand on my mother or me," he says. Yet, "I had no experience of home being a nurturing environment whatsoever." His mother, a hoarder, was emotionally distant while his dad, who worked two jobs—one overnight—and who Christopher rarely saw, had a temper. . . . The problem, as he sees it now at 43, was that both of his parents were suffering from severe depression, undiagnosed and untreated. As a result, he says his home life was anything but a refuge, and his tactic for survival was "to be as quiet and silent as possible." One of Christopher's earliest memories is of waking up crying in his crib after having a nightmare. "No one came. I cried myself back to sleep." . . . The neglect from his parents was compounded further when a neighbor sexually abused him for three years, starting when he was 8 and turning Christopher's world even more upside down. His traumatic childhood eventually lead to addiction, depression, anxiety and thoughts of suicide before Christopher got help in his 30s. For the first time, he says, he admitted the sexual assault and all the adverse effects that followed. A good therapist helped him work through it, but he says the healing is an ongoing process. (domesticshelters.org)

The same formula for creating a compelling victim character is in another story, that of Steven, used in a *Huffington Post* article to demonstrate the dire consequences of a behavior called "bullying." This story, like that of Christopher's, is centered on developing the characteristics qualifying Steven as a victim: He was an indisputably good child, a "sweet, sensitive, artistic" child who "adored his older sister . . . and his dog." He suffered harm because of characteristics both not under his control as well as not justifying his treatment: He was "small" and "awkward" and "didn't quite fit in":

> His name was Steven. He was 13 years old and six years ago, he hung himself in his bedroom closet after being tormented by bullies . . . Steven was a sweet, sensitive and artistic kid. He adored his older sister and he loved skateboarding, baseball, music and his dog, Finster. He also happened to be a little awkward. He was a smallish kid who was different and just didn't quite fit in. To some extent he had always been the target of teasing, but it was in middle school at the beginning of 7th grade when the bullying escalated to a level Steven could no longer face. That day, his tormentors set him on fire with a lighter and an aerosol can of body spray. They recorded their attack on a cell phone and posted it on the Internet. Later that evening while his mom was getting dinner ready, Steven took his own life. (Hewitt 2012)

The Hero Character

Unlike the victim character who is weak, the hero character is strong (Bergstrand and Jasper 2018). Unlike the victim character who requires help, the hero character takes risks to help others (Rankin and Eagly 2008). While both hero and victim characters are evaluated as good people, the hero is superior in morality (Klapp 1954). The emotion code surrounding hero promotes appropriate feelings such as admiration, veneration, and praise, which are expressed in behaviors such as deference or respect.

The likely perceived morality of hero characters can be enhanced by increasing the number of heroic acts. The following story contains two hero characters, both National Guardsmen. While being wounded in the line of duty is more than sufficient to warrant the identity of hero, the morality of these two characters is further enhanced by depicting them as instances of the good American character who does not give up and who remains cheerful. Still further, morality is increased when characters do good deeds for others:

> It was supposed to be a routine patrol for D. B., a National Guardsman serving in northern Iraq. But when the Humvee he was in veered slightly off the road, his life changed in an instant. . . . The vehicle hit an anti-tank land mine, flying nearly 50 feet in the air. When B. came to, his legs were pinned under the wreckage. Within days, both were amputated below the knee. It was a life-altering injury, but from the beginning, B. had a positive attitude about it. He spent a year recovering at Walter Reed Army Medical Center in Washington, and he hoped to build a house for his wife and two young sons when he returned home to Statesville, North Carolina. But given his new reality—two prosthetic legs and, at times, a wheelchair—he wasn't sure how he'd manage it. [The story continues with how his community banded together to help him build a wheelchair accessible home.] Throughout the construction, B. consulted his friend J. G., a building contractor with whom he'd served in the National Guard and was driving the Humvee when it hit the land mine. J.G. suffered a traumatic brain injury in the blast and was later diagnosed with post-traumatic stress disorder. While his wounds were less visible than B.'s, he also struggled to adjust to post-war life. When the house was finished, B. and J.G. decided to "pay it forward" to help other disabled veterans. In 2008, they pooled their military disability payments and started Purple Heart Homes , a nonprofit that so far has modified or helped provide homes for 30 disabled veterans in several East Coast states. (Toner 2013)

While soldiers and first responders risking their physical lives to help others are identities most commonly authored as heroes, the character type is not limited to physically heroic acts because the hero's strength can be intellectual or moral rather than physical (Bergstrand and Jasper 2018). The following story, "Caring," was written by a child. Drawing from a child's understanding of the characteristics of "heroes," this story valorizes a mother's self-sacrifice, establishes her as a hero and a good American who works tirelessly for the good of her family.

> My hero is my mom because she is has done so much and been through so much and she is still the best mom ever, and she would do anything for her

kids! One reason why I chose my mom is because she is strong like batman, just like batman. . . . Also my mom is also like Wonder woman, because they are both strong and they don't back down from challenges, one reason she is like this because she had a stomach ache and she went to work and stayed there because she knew we needed money. She is also a hero because she would do anything for her kids, just to make it so they are okay or if they have enough food for their kids. . . . My mother is a very important person in my life, and she is a very heroic person! (Rasmusen, n.d.)

The Villain Character

In contrast to victim and hero characters who are morally good, the villain character is bad. In comparison to victim characters who experience harm and hero characters who save others from harm, the villain character creates harm. Villain is a symbolic code, a set of evaluations for characters who *create* harm, and who *intend* to create this harm for *no good reason* (Brooks 1976; Loseke 2009; Singer 2001). Emotions associated with the villain character include anger, aversion, disgust, fear, or hatred with punishment as the expected accompanying behavior.

An important sub-type of the villain character is the "evil villain," a character who, in addition to creating great harm, also feels no remorse and derives pleasure from the pain created for others (Alford 1997; Garrard 2002; Lemert 1997). The following story segment is contained in an article, "41 Short Stories of Unforgettable Evil from 41 People." Notice the varieties of activities designated as villainous as well as how the designation of extreme villainy—evil—is reserved for those perceived as downright gleeful about creating great harm for good people. In this story, the immorality of the villain is intensified by elaborating the goodness of one of the victims, a "really great guy" who "ran a charity for Burmese orphans."

I lived in London UK during the riots they had in the summer of 2011. . . . I saw a lot of bad shit that night that made me feel uncomfortable with humanity—a mother holding the metal gate of an off license shop open so that her 9/ 10 year-old could squeeze in and start passing bottles of booze out to her—a herd of women walking into Debenham's empty-handed, then back out with fully-stuffed roller luggage—and people throwing rocks at photographers. But the worst? The absolute worst feeling I ever had was seeing the look of terror on people's faces in the windows of the flats across the road when they realized some looters had set the costume shop beneath their apartments on fire . . . the complete lack of regard for the people living in the apartments above Party Superstore was chilling. I can remember a group of guys coming out of the shop in blank white masks, and one of them had a Jester's hat on, and swayed beneath a street light while watching the shop catch fire. . . . The smell of the fire stuck with me for days. The guy who owned the shop, named Duncan—is a really great guy too. He ran a charity for Burmese orphans. . . . That was a hell of a night. (Koh 2013)

Stock Characters in Socially Circulating Stories

While pure types of victims, villains, and heroes can be found in socially circulating stories, a benefit of the narrative form is its ability to convey the complex, indeterminant, and often contradictory nature of people and experiences. Stories can convey such complexities in several ways.

For example, as in real life where the meanings and evaluations of individual selves can be inextricably bound to social relationships, story characters can derive their individual meanings and evaluations from their *interactions* with other characters. Nowhere is this more common or clearer than in relationships between victim and villain characters. The title of a story, "Jerry Sandusky's 'Victim Four' Tells his Story of Alleged Abuse for Years by Sandusky as a Surrogate Father," draws attention to the family-type relationship between the abuser and the abused. The story *simultaneously* produces Sandusky's villainy and the victim's innocence:

> Victim Four met Jerry Sandusky when he was 12 or 13. . . . Sandusky was kind to the boy, and initially Victim Four thrived on the affection. . . . The two started working out together, playing sports together. The boy accompanied Sandusky to charity events, parties and on football trips. . . . Now 27, Victim Four was a fixture in the Sandusky household as a child. And Sandusky, the youth's attorney says, played two roles—that of a father and that of a molester. "He had a very close relationship with Mr. Sandusky, and I think his relationship was similar to a familial relationship and I think that's part of the reason it was initially so hard for my client to come forward," said Andreozzi, of Harrisburg, who also represents another man who says he was molested by Sandusky. "He viewed him almost as a family member and he looked up to him because there were some things that Jerry was doing positive at the time." (Ganin 2011)

Another example is "Running for her Life," where the villain becomes enraged when his deaf wife does not hear his demands. Victimizing her because of her disability increases his villainy. Simultaneously, her moral purity is increased by emphasizing her good American character attribute of relentless efforts to "keep going" despite hardship:

> One night in November of 2015, Danielle's husband came home drunk and ready to argue. Because of her hearing impairment, she couldn't understand what he was saying. It enraged him. Danielle tried to leave—that's when her husband pulled out a gun and shot her through the chest. "I think it was just pure adrenalin and the will to live that made me get out of the house. I honestly thought he would shoot me in the back as I was trying to get the door open," she says. . . . Danielle spent two weeks in the hospital recovering from a collapsed lung, broken ribs, a broken sternum and a lacerated lung. Her husband went to jail and is still awaiting trial. "After I got back home, something inside of me said, 'This is not going to stop me,'" says Danielle. She credits

herself as being very strong willed, and was determined she would run again. She began by walking a little each day. "It took me a month to be able to walk a mile." From there, she began to walk two miles. Her determination never wavered. . . . This year, she'll participate in the largest 15K race in the U.S. Danielle says she still has chronic pain from her injuries, as well as bullet fragments in her chest. "But it won't stop me from running." (DomesticShelters.org)

Another way that story characters can convey the complexity of lived experience is by character *change over time*. "Villain and Back Again: The Chris Herren Story" is about a character who initially is both villain (using illegal enhancement drugs in sports competitions) and victim (trying to meet unrealistically high social expectations). The story is about his movement from villain/victim to hero now living in a state of grace as a drug-free husband, father, mentor, and coach:

Chris Herren . . . was an incredibly gifted basketball player . . . playing for the team he idolized growing up, the famed and storied Boston Celtics. . . . The pressure of living up to such great expectations was far too much. So Herren coped the only way he knew how—by using drugs. . . . After hitting bottom and becoming the villain, Herren wound up choosing to lean right into the pain and he faced his demons. In doing so, there is perhaps a demonstration of a greater sense of heroism than he ever had playing basketball . . . Herren has been sober since 2008 and fights on, but does so with a caution. . . . Chris Herren lost the fame and fortune that basketball would have brought him. He was once the beloved hero of his community for being the shining star and local boy made good. He fell from grace. In getting back up off the canvas, however, he became a much greater example of what it means to be human. He is a husband, father, and recovering drug addict. Most importantly, he takes each day to face his past and help others in the process as a mentor and a coach. That is a hero. (Stevens, n.d.)

Stories also can convey real world complexity by explicitly including details leading to victim or villain designations. The following story, "Is Angelina Jolie the real villain in her divorce with Brad Pitt?" is centered on elaborating the ways in which Brad Pitt is *not* a *villain* and the ways in which Angelia Jolie is *not* a *victim*:

Brad Pitt has finally won some sympathy after his split from Angelina Jolie. We all know that the superstar couple did not have an amicable split when Jolie filed for divorce last year. But finally, after they settled the feud that lasted for months, they decided to reach out and talk again for the best of their six children. Now, the latest reports are claiming that Jolie has been making her ex the villain in their separation, but Pitt seems to be in a better position than her in the eyes of the public. E! News noted that after their split, Jolie's life seemed less transformed than Pitt, while the Allied star went through a major mid-life reinvention. In fact, he started a new hobby: sculpting. On the other hand, Jolie continued with the same routine and wears the same monochrome outfits and barely-there makeup.

Additionally, during Pitt's interview with GQ, he talked about the sudden transition of being a husband and father to being single, which Jolie missed in her interviews, reported Yahoo! In fact, the *Changeling* star did not seem to be in touch with other single moms. Prior to this, many believed that Jolie has been making Pitt the bad guy. For instance, she claimed that he wanted to seal the divorce documents because he was "terrified that the public will learn the truth." In addition, a source claimed that Jolie was "making him [Pitt] out to be the villain" in her interview with Vanity Fair in September when the actress implied that the children are healing from him. (*Express Tribune* 2017)

Story characters also can attest to life's irony. The following story starts with identifying Dan M. as a member of the highly respected identity category of Marine. The story details his heroism as a Marine, and contains events showing how Dan M. had dedicated his life as a veteran to helping other veterans. In multiple ways, he is a good person and a hero. The story is ironic because the villain who killed Dan M. also was a Marine:

If Dan M. were alive, his friends believe he'd be wondering what he could have done for the former Marine who walked into a crowded bar and started shooting. Instead, M., 33, who also served in the Marines, was one of 12 to die Wednesday night in the shooter's spray of bullets at the Borderline Bar and Grill. Friends and family said he died trying to protect others—something he did every day as an advocate for veterans. The former field radio operator served in the Marines from 2003 to 2007, including a 2007 deployment to Iraq, federal authorities confirmed. He rose to the rank of sergeant and earned multiple awards. In 2012, an old friend and fellow veteran, J. P., asked M. if he wanted to join the Ventura County chapter of Team Red, White and Blue, an organization that offers veterans a sense of community. M. immediately said yes. By the next year, she said, he was chapter president. It was a volunteer position that he eagerly filled. Nearly every weekend for five years, Manrique would organize events for area veterans, including bowling nights and an annual workshop to teach disabled veterans to surf. They helped veterans used to military camaraderie settle more easily into life back home. If M. had survived, Air Force veteran R. F. said, he would have asked, "How could we have helped him? . . . The biggest irony," he said, "is that the people he wanted to help ended up turning a gun on him." (Kohli and Santa Cruz 2018)

In conclusion, socially circulating stories contain individual and/or categorical characters who can be understood as instances of particular identities. Although the pure types of the most common characters are a typical feature of socially circulating stories, an important power of the narrative form is its flexibility and ability to convey social relationships, complexity, change over time, and irony.

All of this is important for a practical reason: The world of troubled meaning creates identity as a problem. American psychologists and sociologists have been most interested in exploring how individuals create self-stories that answer the "who am I?" question.

SELF-STORIES AND MEANING-MAKING

Many scholars have noted that characteristics of modern industrial or postindustrial societies make it difficult for social actors to achieve and maintain a sense of personal identity (Calhoun 1994; Duany 1998; MacIntyre 1984; McAdams 1996). Regardless, psychological well-being depends upon having an answer to the "who am I" question, and most people most of the time do manage to obtain an adequate sense of self. The basic question is: How can a relatively coherent sense of identity be achieved and maintained within a world that is nonsupportive of, or even antagonistic to, such coherence?

An important route to identity creation and maintenance is a "self story," which is a story authored by the self featuring the self as the main character and self-experiences as story events. Rather than seeing a life as simply "one damned thing after another," self-stories allow the creation of coherence (K. Gergen 1994, 187), the possibility of "linking diverse life events into unified and meaningful wholes" (Polkinghorne 1991, 136), the chance to integrate a "reconstructed past, perceived present and anticipated futures in terms of beginnings, middles, and endings" (McAdams 1996, 298).

Challenges in Authoring Self-Stories

Creating adequate self-stories is difficult for several reasons. For example, while such stories are uniquely owned by the story author, to be evaluated as believable, self-stories must at least partially reflect the kinds of stories that prevail in the culture in which they are evaluated (Alcoff and Gray 1993; Bruner 1987; Maines 1991; Riessman 1992). As stated by Jerome Bruner (1987, 15):

> [S]tory authors can not write any story they desire because, just as stories are social in their uses and consequences, they are social in their contents, meanings, and evaluations. Cultures—both local and writ large—define what is, and what is not, an acceptable story.

Characteristics of personal experiences in the current era create other problems for authoring self-stories. Adequate self-stories, for instance, make sense of personal experiences in the past *and* present *and* anticipated future which is difficult when social environments and individual lives are characterized by constant movement and change. Further, given heterogeneity, many self-stories are evaluated as adequate by some audiences to them and as not adequate by others.

Practical actors must create self-stories that are logical and deemed adequate within multiple cultural, social, and practical constraints. It is remarkable that, despite such constraints, most people most of the time do possess self-stories that they and others around them evaluate as adequate. Socially circulating stories are an important tool in authoring such a story.

Socially Circulating Stories and Self-Stories

The social world contains a "milieu of multiple narratives" (Gergen and Gergen 1983, 263), an "ever proliferating catalog of new stories" (Weeks 1998, 460) that can be used as resources for writing self-stories. Indeed, the stories of others can be *explicitly* promoted as such resources. The description on Amazon.com of a self-help book of "true stories" about overcoming opioid addiction informs readers that "by hearing the stories of recovering opioid addicts . . . you can begin to imagine how to overcome opioid addiction"; an Oprah Winfrey show (May 3, 2006) featured one woman who told her personal story of extreme violence. Oprah instructed her audience members who were "living with abuse" to take this story as "classic" and to interpret the meanings of their own experiences in its terms.

Considerable evidence shows that people experiencing troubles such as grave illness (Frank 1995), marginalized sexualities (Plummer 1995), and relationship troubles (Irvine 1999) actively scan the environment for stories that might make sense of personal experiences. There also is evidence that people use socially circulating stories to understand their own experiences and selves: Women who are raped often base their understandings of their own experiences on the "classic rape" story (Wood and Rennie 1994); women experiencing violence know how they "should" respond to this violence because of their awareness of the socially circulating "abused woman" story (Baker 1996; Riessman 1989, 1992). Personal stories of celebrities experiencing medical problems also can lead individuals to take the medical steps promoted by the stories (Chapman et al. 2005; Dubriwny 2009; Metcalf, Price, and Powell 2010).

That said, the process of finding a story capable of being appropriated as one's own is not easy because there commonly are multiple—often contradictory—socially circulating stories from which to choose. Further, many socially circulating stories likely will be evaluated as not pertaining because the characteristics leading particular stories to be widely circulating and hence available to large audiences are the *same* attributes preventing their general usefulness as models for self-stories. That is, the most popular and widely circulating stories often exclude the experiences and views of marginalized and disadvantaged population segments (Mischler 1995); to be widely known, stories must spread through media which simultaneously reduces story complexity while dramatizing story contents (Schudson 1989); the most widely circulating stories tend to feature stock characters and clear plots while most people, and most experiences, are not so clear. In consequence, while socially circulating stories are a resource to make sense of self and experiences, not all stories are useful. Stories diverging too much from practical experience are simply *rejected* as not pertaining; stories denying the evaluator's conception of self will be actively *resisted* (for example, Barcelos and Gubrium 2014; Cohen 1997; Ferrence 2012; Fisher 1984; Hancock 2004; Kirkman et al. 2001; Seccombe et al. 1998).

To summarize, while individuals author self-stories, and while socially circulating stories are a critical meaning-making resource for this task, the actual process of authoring stories is contingent, complex, and ongoing. On a case-by-case basis, people piece together self-stories by outright rejecting some possible stories, and by selecting and modifying fragments from others in ways reflecting their practical experience, commonsense, and moral evaluations. In this way, each self story simultaneously is personal and social, unique and standard.

STORIES AND MAKING SENSE OF OTHERS

Negotiating social life requires some understandings of what to expect from, as well as how to think and feel about and act toward others. While *known* others can be understood and reacted to on the basis of personal experiences, there are many people encountered in daily life—clerks and restaurant servers, customers, those on public transportation—where there is no alternative but to rely on images of *categories* of people. Often such images come in the form of socially circulating stories. Anthropologists argue that socially circulating stories implicitly provide hypotheses about what to expect from unknown others, and there is considerable empirical research that these expectations filter perceptions so that people are prone to see and hear what is anticipated (D'Andrade 1995).

Observers have been most interested in exploring how socially circulating stories lead people in marginalized identity categories to be evaluated by strangers as morally deficient in face-to-face interactions. So, for example, white employers can filter their perceptions of African-American women workers through the popular story of such women as "single mothers." Doing so is associated with assuming such a woman will have responsibilities for childcare and therefore will not be a good employee (Kennelly 1999). In the same way, women relying on welfare (Hancock 2004; Seccombe et al. 1998), mothers who are teens (Kirkman et al. 2001), and people who eat in soup kitchens (Cohen 1997) talk passionately about how unknown others automatically respond to them as individual instances of the morally deficient categorical characters of the "welfare mother," the "teen mother," the "poor."

In a world saturated with media produced images, strangers in daily life also include those known only as images on screens. Primarily an ever-changing assortment of villains and victims, such stories can be packaged as news or human interest; they might be in the service of gaining votes or donations, to support efforts to help or punish. Stories might be organized in ways encouraging audiences to feel anger or fear or sympathy or compassion. In the world of troubled meaning, it is common for multiple stories to circulate simultaneously. Throughout United States history, for example, there have been two opposing stories of immigration. The immigrant as villain story currently dominates in the United States and includes stories of the "Latina Threat" (Chavez 2008), "Mexican Threat" (Aguirre, Rodriguez, and Simmers 2011), and "Syrian Refugee Threat." In sharp contrast is the counter story of immigrants as victims (of oppressive regimes, of war, of famine) seeking only an opportunity to be a part of the American Dream (Edwards and Herder 2012).

AN ILLUSTRATION: THE GOOD AMERICAN CHARACTER AND EVALUATIONS OF SELF AND OTHERS

In the last chapter I argued that the *story* of the American Dream is a cultural resource that can do important work by providing models of how the world does and should work. In the same way, and inextricably related, the good American *character* is a cultural resource.

The good American character can be used as a yardstick to evaluate *morality*, which in turn, can become a justification for *social hierarchy*: As a yardstick of morality, the good American character encourages evaluating those who work as morally superior to those who do not (Sherman 2009). Yet the simple fact of employment is not sufficient: The good American character is moral through and through. Hence, others deemed not so moral can be devalued. Consider the following in which a company owner is talking with a researcher about part time workers who steal from his company. This becomes an issue of moral evaluation. He separates part-time workers into two categories. There are those ("they") who are immoral and the ways in which they are immoral are the ways in which they deviate from the good American character: They aren't committed to work because "all they are interested in is making money." Rather than working for their family members, they want money so they can "drink or smoke." Further, unlike good people who are at home at night, these morally suspect workers stay out all night and we know because "they're wearing the same clothes." Critically, they do not have self-respect ("they're looking for you to buy them cigarettes or breakfast or lunch"). Compare this to his second category of part-time workers, the "good guys," the "decent guys" making a "couple of extra bucks" at night which invites audiences to assume these men have other jobs:

> All they are interested in is making money for the day, so they can drink or smoke it, or whatever they do with it. And they come back the next day, lots of times, some of them, not all of them, but some of them, they're wearing the same clothes and they were out all night and they don't have any money and the next morning they're looking for you to buy them cigarettes or breakfast or lunch or whatever . . . but there are some guys that come down that work nights to make a couple of extra bucks on the side, and they're decent guys, they're good guys to work with. (Quoted in Lamont 2000a, 138)

Another man talking with the researcher reflects on his own social standing by comparing himself to others. Although he says he does not feel superior to these others, he admits he "felt better about himself" after making this comparison. In this case, the criteria for making this evaluation was clothing:

> I went to one of my wholesale distributors yesterday. I was inside and I was who I am, jacket and tie and everything, and I understood that they were interviewing for a warehouse job or whatever. I saw all these guys coming in, that were wearing jeans and sneakers and everything else and I just thought that I used to be in that position. I used to be there and look at who I am now. But still I don't feel superior over that guy, but I felt better about myself when I looked at them because I was there. (Quoted in Lamont 2000a, 98)

Given that the images of the good American character can be used as a yardstick to evaluate self and others, it is not surprising that people crafting self-stories explicitly—and even dramatically—author themselves as instances of this character. This is particularly so for people requiring the assistance of others, which defies the moral value of self-sufficiency. The following story is contained on a website seeking donations to reduce hunger in the United States. Candy authors herself, her husband, and her aging parents as instances of the good American character. Her story is tightly focused on how their need for assistance is *not* the result of bad choices or bad behaviors. On the contrary, Candy's self-story is about how she and her family members are good people despite requiring assistance: Her parents "worked their entire lives," her husband "works full time." Despite hardship, this is a good American family: You do not turn away from family members in need; she and her husband "skip meals" so her parents can eat. This story invites audience members to evaluate Candy and her family as worthy of both sympathy and donations:

> When your loved ones need you, you can either turn away or choose to help. My name is Candy, and I chose to help. Currently, I live with and take care of

my aging parents. I am actually married with three children—ages 13, 14 and 18—but my parents require 24-hour care, so I stay with them while the rest of my family lives next door. A few years ago, my father was diagnosed with Alzheimer's. It's gotten to the point where he no longer remembers anyone and can't do anything for himself. My mother's health is failing as well. She doesn't have the ability to care for him, so the responsibility is on me. My parents worked their entire lives, but through no fault of their own they've been left with only a small, fixed income. Consequently, it's fallen on my family to help provide for them. My husband works full time, but with seven mouths to feed now it's barely enough to get by. We've often had to choose between buying food and medicine, and sometimes, my husband and I skip meals altogether so my parents can eat. (Feeding America, n.d.)

The pervasiveness of the American Dream story theme and characters makes it an especially important resource for making sense of self and others. As with all identities, the good American—and its binary opposite of the not good American—comes with a constellation of expectations, rights, obligations, moral evaluations, and opportunities.

Because the good American character is the most prized character in the United States, it follows that people whose motivations and behaviors can be evaluated as those of this type might experience particular constellations of emotions such as pride in being a character so highly valued, joy when success is achieved for self and family, perhaps self-satisfaction for the high standing in the moral hierarchy (Lauby 2016). Yet because this character is responsible for both its own successes and failures, it disguises structural foundations of individual success and encourages disadvantaged people, such as poor immigrants (McGinnis 2009; Nicholls and Fiorito 2015) and gay men (Jackson 2012) to blame themselves for any lack of success they experience.

NARRATIVES AND IDENTITY: BEYOND INDIVIDUAL MEANING-MAKING

American psychologists and sociologists have focused their attention on a variety of social psychological questions about how practical actors create, maintain, and use self-stories in ways answering the important question, "Who am I?" (Frank 1995; Holstein and Gubrium 2012; McAdams 1996). While a large number of empirical studies attest to the richness of this line of research, this tradition can be criticized for giving too little attention to the social and political *contexts* within which self-stories are created, told, and evaluated (Atkinson and Delamont 2006; Gubrium and Holstein 2002). Similarly, a typical interest in exploring the fullness and complexity of personal experience can lead to little attention devoted to relationships between self processes and political processes in self-stories (Clough 2000). Research on self-stories could be enhanced by more sustained attention to the social and political contexts and determinants of story production, story consumption, and story evaluation.

While appreciating the insights offered by examinations of self-stories, the presence of narratives in social life is not limited to self-stories; the work of narratives is not limited to questions about individual psychology. On the contrary: A globalized, mass-mediated, heterogeneous, morally fragmented world creates multiple problems of meaning in *public* life. Narrative is a central tool useful for creating meaning, for creating meaning that persuades and justifies in public arenas, for creating meaning with very tangible practical consequences.

Chapter Four

Narrative and Social Problems

In a world of so much misery, how can people decide which of many conditions creating harm can be ignored and which must be fixed and deserve public resources to do so? How can people decide which of countless victims can be ignored and which should be offered public compassion and material help? Answers to such questions depend upon "social problem consciousness," a cognitive, emotional, and moral evaluation that an intolerable condition exists and requires public resources for its resolution. Social problem consciousness must be *created* because

> [h]uman problems do not spring up, full-blown and announced, into the consciousness of bystanders. Even to recognize a situation as painful requires a system for categorizing and defining events. (Gusfield 1981, 3)

Creating social problem consciousness in heterogeneous audiences requires *persuasion*, and stories are central in this process because persuasion is best accomplished through appealing to both hearts and minds. Exploring the persuasive potentials of stories in creating social problem consciousness differs from looking at how stories help answer questions about identities of self and others: It moves discussion from *private* to public realms, and from *personal* to *political* uses of stories.

SOCIAL PROBLEMS IN A FRAGMENTED WORLD

Consider the following story as evidence of a puzzle:

> December, 2012: A man walks into an elementary school in Newtown, Connecticut USA and guns down 20 six- and seven-year-old children and six teachers. There is a united definition of the event: This is evil, this is horrify-

ing, this is a massacre of the innocents. Many people having no personal ties to the victims nonetheless travel great distances to attend the funerals of the young children; the *Wall Street Journal* reports that this event was so emotionally devastating it decreased Christmas shopping throughout the United States.

From time to time enormous numbers of people sharing little in the way of practical experiences or world views nonetheless agree on the cognitive, moral, and emotional meanings of events lying outside their personal experiences. Understanding events not personally experienced by self or known others *must* come from public communication. How can public communication encourage particular ways of thinking, feeling, and moral evaluation that lead to social problem consciousness?

The social landscape is littered with conditions creating harm ranging from climate change, crumbling infrastructure, terrorism, and poverty to opiate addiction, obesity, and teen pregnancy. Such a variety of conditions can be categorized as specific instances of one thing—social problem—because "social problem" (or "social issue") is a cultural code. As a *symbolic* code, social problem is a term for conditions evaluated as intolerable and in need of change because they unfairly and greatly harm a large number of good people. As such, "social problem" is a summary label for cognitive evaluations of size (widespread), morality (wrong), and required action (need for change). Social problem also is an *emotion* code encouraging some variation of outrage or at least concern for troublesome conditions, some variation of sympathy for those harmed, some variation of condemnation for those creating harm.

How can relatively large population segments concur that a particular condition must be changed when there is no agreement about what is—and what is not—intolerable, about who does—and who does not—deserve help or punishment? The answers to such questions have significant *practical* implications: Social problems in democratic societies are matters of public concern because they are about the allocation of communal resources, both emotional (sympathy or condemnation) and physical (material help or punishment). The answers to such questions also are of *symbolic* consequence because designated victims, villains, and heroes implicated in social problems are placed in particular social and moral hierarchies: Help is offered to those evaluated as honorable; punishment comes to those evaluated as dishonorable (Schneider and Ingram 1993).

The practical question is about persuasion: How are significant numbers of people persuaded that a morally intolerable condition exists and must be changed?

SOCIAL PROBLEMS AND PERSUASION

Rarely is a condition so obviously intolerable that audiences overwhelmingly agree on its meanings. Because publics must be persuaded to think and feel in particular ways, social problem consciousness is a consequence of effective persuasion.

The features and techniques of persuasive communication have been explored by scholars from antiquity to the present. Aristotle, for example, maintained that such communication depends upon inextricably related appeals to logos (logic), ethos (morality), and pathos (emotion). Modern observers have confirmed such age-old reflections when they argue that "cognitive beliefs about how the world is, our moral vision of how the world should be, and our emotional attachment to that world march in close step" (Jasper 1997, 108). Some observers go further in diminishing the importance of logic in persuasion by arguing that escalating public disagreements about what constitutes "truth" have led to relativizing truth and increasing the importance of emotion so that what is *felt* can be more important in shaping understandings and behaviors than what is *thought* (McCarthy 1989, 2017; Loseke and Kusenbach 2008).

Persuading general publics to develop social problem consciousness requires an effective "public moral argument" (Fisher 1984; Jasper 1992). Such arguments are *public* because they are made to general audiences; such arguments are *moral* because they are about fundamental issues of social order, such as who is valued and who is despised or about the rights and obligations of citizenship. As with all persuasion, effective public moral arguments must appeal to logic and emotion, to hearts and minds. Because this is what the narrative form can do, stories are an important tool to encourage social problem consciousness:

> A substantial body of evidence attests to the power of narratives to change attitudes, beliefs, and behaviors. Narrative persuasion has a wide variety of applications, from combating stereotypes to promoting health behaviors. Indeed, narratives might be especially effective under conditions in which individuals might otherwise resist persuasion. (Nabi and Green 2015, 138–139)

Storytelling and Social Movements

Persuasion is the goal of social movements; storytelling is the primary tool for this task. Indeed, so important are stories to the work of social movements that narratives have been called a foundational characteristic of movements for social change (Davis 2002; Fine 2002; Mayer 2014; Polletta 2006). Stories are central to public moral arguments. Stories help recruit new members and convince current activists to continue working despite apparent failures (Beckwith 2014; Davis 2002; Loseke 2003; Mayer 2014; Polletta

1997; Powell 2011). Stories are a critical resource whether activism is about organizing students in the United States in the 1960s (Polletta 2006) modern day mobilizations in Russia, Georgia, or Ukraine (Carnaghan 2016), movements on behalf of abortion rights in Argentina (Borland 2014), those promoting domestic violence legislation in the United States (Lehrner and Allen 2008), or managing censorship of Arab Spring protests in China (Du 2016).

Social movement activists do a great deal of "character work," defined as "efforts to shape the reputations of strategic players into familiar types of protagonists" (Jasper, Young, and Zuern 2018, 114). Character work includes advancing images of the morality of social movement actors, as well as dramatizing how particular people or categories of people involved in social problems are instances of the narrative characters of victims, villains, or heroes.

An excellent example of character work is in the "undocumented youth" movement (Milkman 2014) which has been organized around the first-person testimonies of young adults originally brought to the United States when they were children (Carrasco and Seif 2014). In this case, the story of the American Dream is the central organizing device for the stories told by such undocumented youth. Their self-stories dramatize these youth as "dreamers," a type of person who, although undocumented, is fully assimilated, explicitly and strongly embraces the American values of work and self-sufficiency, dreams of the opportunity to succeed on their own merits, and loves America (Jeffries 2009; Lauby 2016; Milkman 2014). By cultural logic, this character is deserving of inclusion so should be allowed to remain and given opportunities to become a citizen. The self-stories of Alberto and Rocio, on a social advocacy website promoting support for federal legislation protecting such people, demonstrate this story form. Alberto defines himself as a New Yorker and focuses on his hard work and status as a "proud taxpayer":

> My name is Alberto; I am a Dreamer in many forms. I am living and want to continue living the American Dream. I consider myself a New Yorker in every way. New York has given me opportunities that many take for granted. A proud tax payer, working hard on my goals. Working to become part owner of an American company. I live for the American dream and will always be a Dreamer.

Rocio's self-story centers on describing the ways in which his childhood was American in the smallest of ways and how he now is a professional working in one of the offices he and his father had once cleaned:

> I grew up in East Palo Alto, in the heart of Silicon Valley, before and after the dot.com bubble. . . . I watched Star Trek Voyager, Friends, read Dr. Seuss and memorized musicals from Funny Girl to the Wizard of Oz. On the weekends, I helped my dad clean office buildings. I picked up the trash and refilled the

trash can with bags at every room. Today, I am in one of those conference rooms whiteboarding with engineers and product managers to solve the toughest problems in Big Data. (Dreamer Stories, 2018)

In a world of contested meanings, stories appealing to thinking, feeling, and moral evaluation can be powerful resources for encouraging social problem consciousness in large, heterogeneous populations. Not every story, though, is persuasive.

THE SOCIAL PROBLEM FORMULA STORY

Heterogeneity and moral fragmentation lead to the likelihood that any particular condition will be the topic of multiple stories that differ remarkably from one another in their plots, characters, and morals. Such fragmentation, however, typically exists *within* a particular story genre I will call a "social problem formula story." This narrative is a formula because, whether about factory closings or child abuse, about human trafficking or bullying, the story has a particular kind of content that encourages social problem consciousness.

Social problem formula stories feature *plots* dramatizing the devastating harm suffered by good victims. Such characters and plots lead to predictable *morals*: The condition must be changed. Critically, while social problems are about *conditions* creating harm, formula stories most often are *character driven* and dramatize how the primary story character is an exemplar victim:

> Ellie S., 84, uses a wheelchair and public buses to go to her monthly cancer treatments. Starting Sunday, her life will get harder. HART (local bus system) is overhauling its entire network. . . . Stops will move. Times will change. . . . "I heard this was coming, but I had no idea it would be this bad," Mrs. S. said after a *Tampa Bay Times* reporter explained the changes to the 84-year old as she waited for her next bus. "I don't know what I'm going to do." (Johnson 2017)

This one-character story introduces a newspaper article about a particular condition, "changes in bus schedules," that becomes a problem because of the harm these changes create for bus riders. What audiences learn about this character is she uses a wheelchair and has no alternatives to using public transportation and that she uses public transportation to reach her cancer treatments. Audiences are twice told she is 84 years old. Notice how *nothing* in this story might lead audiences to evaluate this character as not a good person, to wonder if her problems are of her own creation, or if she could resolve the problems herself. *Everything* in this story encourages audiences to view her as a sympathy-worthy victim. The story ends emotionally with her helplessness, as she tells readers, "I don't know what I'm going to do." Appealing more to feeling than to thinking, this story encourages audiences to evaluate "changes in bus schedules" as creating great harm. Audiences also are encouraged to assume that this *particular* woman adequately represents a *category* of person—the "bus rider."

In daily life, on a case-by-case basis, people use vastly different criteria to evaluate moral worth, complicity in creating troubles, and extent of harm. Such differences, of course, lead to different evaluations of victim status and therefore, of sympathy worthiness. Social problem formula stories circumvent such practical issues by *dramatizing* both the extensiveness of harm and the purity of victims. Hence, the most widely circulating stories of child abuse feature barbaric violence toward babies and toddlers (not "slapping" a teen son who stole and crashed the family car), just as stories of unemployment feature characters with long histories of heroic labor who now are out of jobs and destitute (not those whose relationship to the workforce always has been tenuous). Stories of extreme suffering by indisputably innocent people circumvent the practical problems of evaluating particular conditions that can seem not so awful, and particular people who can seem not so saintly.

Victim characters in social problem formula stories tend to be variations of the good American character. Consider, for example, a story introducing an article asking readers to support the United Nations World Food Program. The central character, 10-year old Ro, works tirelessly and endlessly to buy food for his parents and three siblings. Although Ro lives in India, he nonetheless is an instance of the good American character which encourages American audiences to admire his goodness and, in response, to support a program making his life a bit easier:

> So, every day for the past few weeks, Ro has gone to the banks of the Gandak river with magnetic rings tied to the end of a fishing pole. The reason? To try to fish coins out the water, that have been thrown into the river by visitors during a huge month-long fair. And he doesn't just go for a few minutes. He puts in a 12-hour day, from 5am to 5pm—which means he's not in school. He's missing classes for a month, to help his family get by. Any money Ro finds, he gives to his parents so they can get enough food for he and his three siblings. (Stroumboulopoulos 2012)

Social problem formula stories almost always contain a victim character—without a victim there is no problem—and these stories often are tightly focused on this character. The second type of character is the *villain*, a character who rarely is of central importance and who often is completely absent: Neither the stories of Ro or Ellie S. feature a villain. When villain characters are a part of the story they often are undeveloped. The following story about the problem of "phantom debt" contains an extremely detailed portrait of Andrew, the victim. The story describes his physical appearance, personality, work, home. While audiences know from the story opening that the villain is the "debt collector" who threatened to rape Andrew's wife, this character is not developed and the emotionally persuasive power of the story comes from the victimization of Andrew, a good American character who works hard, cares for his family, is not responsible for his troubles and, therefore, deserves sympathy:

> On the morning a debt collector threatened to rape his wife, Andrew was working from home, in a house with green shutters on a cul-de-sac in a small Rhode Island town. Tall and stocky, with a buzz cut and a square, friendly face, Andrew was a salesman for a promotions company. He'd always had an easy rapport with people over the phone, and on that day, in February 2015, he was calling food vendors to talk about grocery store giveaways. He was interrupted . . . by a call from his wife. She'd gotten a voicemail from an authoritative-sounding man saying Andrew was in some kind of trouble. . . . [He] had been caught up in a fraud known as phantom debt, where millions of Americans are hassled to pay back money they don't owe. (Faux 2017)

Although villain *characters* can be missing or undeveloped, the *consequences* of villainy in social problem formula stories can be dramatized through emphasizing the purity and suffering of victims. The central theme in the following story, from the Mothers Against Drunk Driving (MADD) website, is the goodness of the immediate victim, a police officer. As developed in the story, this goodness is unquestionable: He always dreamed of being a police officer; he "saved people's lives," he was killed while helping a stranded motorist—and the motorists' child. The pathos is multiple: He was killed "just a few months after being sworn in," he was "young," his death was "senseless;" his family still grieves 25 years later. All audiences learn about the villain drunk driver is that this character is male ("he") who served 15 years in prison, far less time than a mother has anguished over the death of her son.

> For Joyce W. September 1st 1992, marks a day that she will never forget. For 25 years she has experienced the grief caused by the drunk driving crash that killed her oldest son, Officer Brent W. of the Fort Worth Police Department. . . . At the age of 22, Officer W. began fulfilling his dream when he graduated from the Fort Worth Police Academy. Just a few months after being sworn in, Officer W. was on duty when he saw a motorist and his 14 year old son on the side of the road experiencing car trouble. Without hesitation, Officer W. offered his assistance. He parked his patrol unit behind the car and began changing a flat tire when a vehicle struck him from behind and pinned him in between both cars. Officer W. died a hero. . . . He saved people's lives. . . . Twenty five years have passed since the life of a young police officer was taken in a senseless crime. The drunk driver was convicted of involuntary manslaughter and sentenced to fifteen years in prison. He has served his sentence, while Joyce and her family continue to think of Brent wherever they go. (Mothers Against Drunk Driving 2017)

A third character that might be expected in social problem formula stories is the *hero* who rights the wrongs. Yet stories rarely contain such a character and this makes sense: Heroes solve problems, so if a story has a hero there is no problem to be resolved. What stories often do contain are promises that audiences can *produce* heroes—typically in the form of social policies and social services—if they support efforts to change the condition producing harm.

CHARACTER COMPETITIONS IN FORMULA STORIES

Given heterogeneity and moral fragmentation, public moral arguments about social problems often feature story competitions. As would be expected given the centrality of the cultural code of individualism, it is common for competitions about *conditions* creating harm to be transformed to competitions about *characters*.

An Illustration: Competing Stories About Immigration and Undocumented Immigrants

The condition of "immigration" has at least two formations as a social problem: Some people evaluate the condition as a problem of the less-than-welcoming treatment suffered by those entering the United States without documentation; others evaluate the condition as a problem of too easy entry to the United States. Public moral arguments supporting the cognitive, emotional, and moral rightness of each of these images can be accomplished by authoring immigrants as particular types of people deserving either inclusion or exclusion.

Stories supporting calls for making the United States more welcoming to immigrants typically feature characters who are the good American type of person—despite a lack of legal documentation. Felix G. is one such exemplary person who has "played by the rules," worked hard, achieved success, taught his children both the importance of education and of volunteering to help others. A second character, his daughter, Belsy, likewise is a distinctly good American who is graduating from medical school and wants to help those in "underserved communities." These stories are powerful justifications for policies that would allow these characters to remain in the United States.

> This should be one of the proudest moments of Felix G.'s life. His eldest daughter, Belsy, has just about one year left before she graduates from [medical school]. Instead, the dad of three is sitting in Immigration and Customs Enforcement (ICE) detention with a deportation date just days away. . . . Lots of people have been talking about undocumented immigrants needing to "fol-

low the rules," and that's exactly what G. had been doing. For seven years, the undocumented dad checked in regularly with ICE, to show that he was working, paying his taxes, and continuing to have a clean record. [Belsy says] "My father considers the United States his home . . . and he is a living example of the American Dream." G. had originally fallen onto ICE's radar in 2011, but under the Obama administration was given annual stays, as long as he continued checking in. "G. felt mostly safe. He started to buy houses, repair them and sell them, and then to buy land and build the houses from the ground up, teaching himself methods on YouTube and employing workers." . . . "[My dad] made us volunteer and he was always about us doing well in school," said Belsy, who faces an uncertain future of her own due to DACA's status. She hopes she can graduate and help underserved communities. (Ortiz 2018)

Conversely, stories featuring immigrants as villains support efforts to make it more difficult to enter the country. Villainy is accomplished by dramatizing the goodness of the American citizen victim:

Roberto G. , an unlicensed driver from Honduras who entered the U.S. illegally . . . killed Drew R., a second-year law student. . . . R. was riding his motorcycle when G. ran over him three times with his car." Also, Sarah R., 21, from Omaha, Nebraska was killed on January 31, 2016. Her SUV was rear-ended by Edwin M., an illegal alien from Honduras, who was street racing. Sarah had just graduated from Bellevue University with a 4.0 GPA the day before she passed away. . . . M. was charged with motor vehicular homicide but posted bond to get out of jail and was released. He is still on the run. (Federation for American Immigration Reform)

An Illustration: Competing Stories of Welfare Recipients

What should be the public responsibility for people not achieving self-reliance in the United States? While interest in this question goes back to the 1700s (Townsend 1786) and has been of cyclical concern throughout the nation's history (Axinn and Levin 1982; Patterson 1981). Answers to questions about public responsibility depend upon answers to another question: Why do people need public assistance? Countless specific reasons for need typically are sorted into two categories reflecting answers to yet another question: Is this character responsible for creating the need (Handler and Hasenfeld 1991; Lamont and Small 2008; Stryker and Wald 2009)? The cognitive, emotional, and moral reasoning needed to answer these questions is enormously complex so cannot be enumerated in bullet points or statistics. Only stories can show the grounds for making such distinctly moral classifications.

Throughout the entire history of the United States there have been two types of competing stories about people needing public assistance. One story features the social welfare recipient as a morally suspect character who is unworthy of public assistance. The narrator in the following, "A Welfare

Story," positions herself as a good American because she is employed in a convenience store. Her story about customers creates a welfare recipient character in explicit detail who symbolizes all that is *not* the good American. This includes a lengthy list of perceived transgressions: This welfare recipient character is rude, overweight, dirty, drinks beer, smokes cigarettes, eats unhealthy food, is irresponsible and lazy and wastes money on expensive phones, manicures, magazines, and lottery tickets. This character lives in a trailer! In appearance, attitudes, motivations, behaviors—and place of residence—the welfare recipient character is the anthesis of the good American who "wants to move up in the world."

> The worst one was a young woman—in her 20s—who was overweight, rude, and unkempt. She did her grocery shopping at our store. Every few days she came in and . . . made a pile on the counter: cold cuts, beef jerky, string cheese, candy bars, chips, bread, hot dogs, a 12-pack or two of soda, and some ice cream bars. This was paid for with her SNAP [Supplemental Nutritional Assistance Program] card. Then we'd ring up her 30-pack of beer, her two or three packs of cigarettes, her tabloid magazine, and $15-$20 worth of lottery tickets. I noticed too that she always had the latest hi-tech phone, and her nails were done in a French manicure. This is no joke—I am not exaggerating. I saw this day in and day out—dozens of people using their SNAP cards to buy junk, and spending their cash on beer, cigarettes, and lottery tickets. Many of these people lived in the trailer park behind the convenience store. . . . Over the years, I discovered that, while some of them were on disability, many of them were not. I'd wonder why they wouldn't want to better their situation and why they didn't save their money—rather than spending it on lottery tickets—and try to move up in the world? The answer: It's easier to stay on welfare. (Kinderman 2016)

It needs no elaboration that such stories promote a particular constellation of cognitive and emotional reactions: Welfare recipients create their own problems and therefore do not deserve sympathy or help.

A second type of story features social welfare recipients as *not* responsible for their need. Such stories focus on the character's desires and relentless effort to achieve independence. The self-story of a 24-year-old contained in an article, "True Stories of Living on the Dole," could be a response to the story told by the convenience store worker. This person is a college graduate who certainly does not live a life of luxury. Rather, the story author works for a government program that pays less than other work because it offers her experience for future jobs as well as help in paying college loans. Certainly such a forward looking person is worthy of a bit of assistance:

> I'm 24. I live in North Carolina. I receive $89 per month in food stamp benefits, and last week, a woman at the grocery store told me I "should be ashamed of [myself]" for paying with EBT (food stamps). When I graduated

from college last year, I spent four months staying with my parents, working a few part-time jobs, and looking for anything that might make use of my degree. I didn't find a "real job," but I did find a position with AmeriCorps in a city four hours away. AmeriCorps VISTA volunteers are placed with community organizations for one year of service and paid a small stipend, and are eligible for a $5,500 award for education expenses upon completion of service. To me, it seemed like the only way to get real work experience, and hopefully pay off some of my student loans while I'm at it. Where I'm serving, my living stipend is around $800 a month. VISTA volunteers are prohibited from holding any other paid employment. I live off of $800 a month, $89 in food stamps . . . I'm getting valuable work experience that I wasn't able to find elsewhere, but I'd make more money working at Walmart. I spend about $650-$700 per month (depending on the season and how much electricity I use) on rent and utilities . . . nothing fancy—I don't have cable, I live in literally the cheapest apartment I could find . . . and I don't have a smartphone. (Nolan 2012)

STORIES OF PERSONAL IDENTITY AS STORIES OF CATEGORICAL IDENTITY

It is common for audiences to be explicitly invited to assume that stories featuring individual characters are adequate representations of stories of types of characters. Consider two stories that are similar in that both are about the social problem of opioid use, feature a woman as the only character, and ask readers to take one woman's story as an exemplar of a typical story.

Audiences are instructed to understand Michele's story as "one of many Floridians who suffer from chronic pain."

> Will Michele J. get out of bed today? That depends on how many painkillers she has left in her monthly prescription, which sometimes she's forced to ration. . . . Michele, 56, has suffered from chronic pain since a 1987 car accident. The county resident has had 73 surgeries since, from her neck to her ankles. . . . In December, she was diagnosed with breast cancer. . . . "I'm not using these drugs to get high. I'm using them so I can have some kind of life . . . so I can get out of bed. They don't take my pain away. But they mask it so I can function." She is one of many Floridians who suffer from chronic pain and are worried about a government crackdown that would make it even harder to get the prescription drugs they need everyday. (Griffin 2018)

Jane's story also is offered as exemplary for she is "like many who get hooked on painkillers":

> When Jane was 14, her father died, sending her into a spiral. She began hanging out with 30-year-old meth users. Without even realizing it, she had begun an addiction. . . . Three years ago, she underwent back surgery and got

hooked on opioids at warp speed. She'd go through a month's worth of prescription pills in a week and scramble to feed her habit for the rest of the
month. She couldn't hold down a job. . . . The opioids provided a high like
she'd never felt. Like many who get hooked on painkillers, she eventually
graduated to heroin, overdosing twice. (Drash 2017)

These two characters are far different: Michele denies opioid addiction; Jane
has "graduated" from painkillers to heroin. While encouraging different
kinds of logical, emotional, and moral evaluations, each of these personal
stories is offered as an exemplar of a category of story, the story of the opioid
user. And so it goes. In a world of heterogeneity and moral fragmentation,
social problems can be represented in multiple ways by deeply contrasting
stories. While questions about which of multiple stories should be accorded
the status of "typical" has an empirical answer (which story most accurately
reflects reality as objectively measured), the story that is the best conveyer of
empirical reality is not necessarily the most effective story for encouraging
social problem consciousness.

EVALUATING THE PERSUASIVENESS OF SOCIAL PROBLEM
FORMULA STORIES

Convincing public moral arguments require persuasion and, because persuasion is most effective when it appeals to both thinking and feeling, public
moral arguments often are saturated with stories. This is, however, a statement of story *potential*. Persuasiveness must be *realized* through evaluations
that take place within environments where stories tend to circulate within
increasingly narrow audience segments; where these segments can have very
different understandings of cultural codes used to evaluate story believability
and importance; where multiple stories on seemingly similar topics offer
widely dissimilar visions of people, experiences, and moralities.

Most obviously, persuasion within such a world is anything but automatic. Phrased in the vocabulary of social media: How is it possible for any
particular story to be "liked," "shared," or "retweeted" enough for it to become available to more than a few people and actually do the work of
creating social problem consciousness? Phrased in terms of persuasiveness:
Which among countless contending stories cognitively, emotionally, and morally persuade more than a few people to evaluate a condition as intolerable
and in need of change? Joel Best (2018, 194) offers a straightforward answer:

[T]hose who want to get people to focus on something need to grab and hold
their attention. This is true for all manner of activities, from individuals trying
to attract likes to their Facebook posts, to television broadcasters competing
for viewers, to activists trying to arouse concern for their causes. These competitions favor those whose messages can grab and hold an audience, and

make people scared or outraged is among the tried-and-true methods of doing this. Moderation and keeping things in perspective make one's claims less competitive.

Story Persuasiveness and Cultural Codes

A story cannot persuade unless it is evaluated as a good story so the persuasive potentials of stories depend upon audience evaluations of story *believability* and *importance*. While believability and importance are judged through comparing a story to personal experience and common sense, such evaluations also depend upon the extent to which story contents reflect evaluators' understandings of *cultural codes* (Davis 2002).

Any social order contains countless cultural codes and these systems of meanings vary in the extent to which they are shared, embraced, and important. Logically, the stories with the most potential to persuade are those incorporating the most widely shared, deeply embraced and central codes (Entman 2003). For example, there are continuing and hotly contested arguments in the United States about the meanings and evaluations of codes surrounding race/ethnicity, citizenship, and sexuality. Stories incorporating such codes are likely evaluated very differently by various audience segments. Other codes—individualism, freedom, family, health—are widely held and deeply embraced so stories incorporating such codes have potentials to be believed and evaluated as important by large segments of general audiences. Persuasiveness is *encouraged* by building stories from the most widely held and deeply embraced cultural codes; persuasiveness is *discouraged* by incorporating contentious codes. Ironically, this means that the most persuasive social problems formula stories will be conservative in that they will be consistent with cultural meanings as understood by the largest and most central population segments.

Story Persuasiveness and Melodrama

The social problems formula story is *melodramatic*, featuring one-dimensional representations of experience and characters, involving plots of struggles between good and evil, and told in a vocabulary of clear and simple moral absolutes (Brooks 1976; Frye 1957; Singer 2001; Wagner-Pacifici 1986). While literary critics deride the melodramatic genre for its simplicity, sensationalism, predictable plot lines, and one-dimensional characters (Brooks 1976; Frye 1957), it is precisely these attributes that lead to story persuasiveness in a world where meaning is troubled. Furthermore, and not to be discounted, because the excessiveness of melodrama can be riveting, this story form is a favorite for media which means such stories will be widely disseminated.

Story Persuasiveness and Meaning-Making in Daily Life

Social problem formula stories achieve their persuasiveness through a melodramatic simplification of a complex, multidimensional world. This recipe increasing story persuasiveness simultaneously reduces the story's value as a meaning-making resource for individuals attempting to make sense of self and others.

For example, while real people are multidimensional, formula story stock characters are one-dimensional *categorical* characters, developed only in ways making them instances of victims or villains. And, although victim characters in formula stories can be saintly and villains can seem all but cartoonish in their evil, actual people often seem more or less virtuous, more or less wicked. In consequence, formula stories can set a very high standard of moral purity to be accorded the status of victim and a very high standard of nastiness to be accorded the status of villain.

Still further, while the world contains many exemplars of the melodramatic *events* featured in formula stories, it contains many more events evaluated as only relatively harmful. This means women using the socially circulating story of the "standard rape" as a template might well evaluate their own experiences or the experiences of others as not so extreme and therefore as "not rape" (Wood and Rennie 1994). When women use socially circulating stories of "intimate partner violence" as a yardstick to evaluate the meanings of their own experience or the experience of others they can decide that particular experiences are "not as bad" as those in the circulating story (Baker 1996). Women methamphetamine users often fail to see themselves in the extreme, melodramatic stories forming the social problem of "meth" (Copes et al. 2015). In such cases, images contained in socially circulating stories seem to not match practical experience so the story is not used as a meaning-making tool. Thus, an irony: The melodramatic "extreme case" formula stories that are so effective in mobilizing public support actually *decrease* the possibilities that social actors will appropriate the story as their own (Gamson 1995; Wood and Rennie 1994; Loseke 2001).

NARRATIVE, SOCIAL PROBLEMS, AND SOCIAL CHANGE

The meaning-making work of stories is achieved through the efforts of people pursuing the practical goals of persuasion. Stories persuade, persuasion is necessary to develop social problem consciousness, social problem consciousness is necessary for social change. Stories are implicated in both types of social change, in the "legislation passed and policies changed," as well as "transformations in culture and consciousness, in collective self-definitions, and in the meanings that shape everyday life" (Polletta 1997, 431).

Transformations in culture and consciousness—subjective change—is most obvious when it involves altering public understandings of cultural codes (Swidler 1995). Many social movements, for example, are characterized as "identity movements," whose goals are to change understandings of the contents and evaluations of particular identity categories such as those surrounding gender, race/ethnicity, sexuality (Bernstein 1997, Brush 1999). Such *subjective* changes in ways of thinking and feeling can yield *material* changes in lives: People in particular categories can experience a change in their position in social hierarchies, they can encounter new sets of expectations, new constellations of opportunities or constraints. Subjective change also can come from education. Considerable research in public health, for example, demonstrates that packaging information in story form leads to stronger cognitive and emotional responses than offering it in the form of simple descriptions (Frank et al. 2015; McQueen et al. 2011; Zebregs et al. 2015). There also is considerable evidence that members of general populations change their own health-related behaviors as a consequence of stories they encounter about celebrity health issues (Dubriwny 2009). In such cases, *subjective* changes in thinking and feeling lead to changes in *behaviors*.

While changing parameters of subjectivity is important for social change, as argued by Anne Kane (2000, 313), "social change also is about explicitly changing the material conditions of social life," which leads to exploring relationships between narrative and public policy.

Chapter Five

Narrative and Social Policy

Within a world characterized by heterogeneity, rapid change, and moral frag-mentation, where meanings are not shared and often hotly contested, how is it possible to create social policy that is supported by relatively large seg-ments of a population? Exploring the place and work of stories in social policy shows how narratives can create meaning, and how that meaning can both *persuade* and *justify* in the public realms of social policy. Further, because policy often leads to concrete changes in the social world (laws, regulations, social services), relationships between narratives and policy demonstrate how stories can be tools for directly shaping *material realities*. As with story meaning-making potentials in encouraging social problem con-sciousness, this is about how narrative is a *political* tool.

I will use the term, social policy, very broadly to include courses of action (or inaction) such as laws, rules, statutes, programs, or procedures, that are accompanied by relatively enforceable systems of rewards and/or punish-ments (Fischer 2003). While businesses make policies influencing employ-ees and customers, social science interest has centered on policy enacted by governments.

NARRATIVE AND THE CULTURAL FOUNDATIONS OF POLICY

Challenges to traditional academic visions of social policy as driven by insti-tutionalized power and elite self-interest started in the 1980s. While certainly not denying the importance of such power and interests, policy studies ex-panded to explore relationships between policy and *culture*. Rather than the conventional conceptualization of culture as mere epiphenomena reflecting material conditions, newer models are of cultural meanings as an *independent* force shaping policy content as well as the process of policy making

(Campbell 2002; Fischer 2003; Jacobs et al. 2003; Lamont and Small 2008; Mazzeo et al. 2003; Padamsee 2009; Pfau-Effinger 2005; Rochefort and Cobb 1994; Stone 1997).

Cultural meanings are central in policy creation and justification. Policies about women, work, and welfare, for example, typically have been justified by constructing how policy supports cultural codes surrounding family and gender as traditionally understood (Asen 2003; Burnstein and Bricher 1997). As a result, cultural ideas valorizing mothering justified the 1935 legislation establishing social welfare (Mazzeo et al. 2003); justifications for the "Violence Against Women's Civil Rights Clause" emphasized the importance of protecting delicate women from victimization (Picart 2003); the symbolic code of family weaves through debates over policies for teen pregnancy (Asen 2003). Obviously, cultural meanings are in the foreground of "morality" policies such as needle exchange programs for addicts, abstinence only sex education, state-sponsored gambling, and so on (Brown 2012; Deeb-Sossa 2007; Olive et al. 2012).

Cultural meaning systems thereby function under the institutionalized power and elite self-interests shaping policy. Within this frame, the essence of the policy process is a struggle over ideas and their meanings:

> Policymaking is a constant discursive struggle over the definitions of problems, the boundaries of categories used to describe them, the criteria for their classifications and assessment, and the meanings of ideas that guide particular actions. (Fischer 2003, 60)

Once again, this leads to narrative because policy debates are political debates, and "political struggle is moral and emotional" (Alexander 2010, xii). Only the narrative form can appeal simultaneously to logic, emotion, and judgments of morality.

Culture and Storytelling in the Policy Process

Testimonies in policy hearings are anything but a "representative" sample of stories that might be told. Rather, what stories might be told is determined by institutionalized power because those in charge of the policy process control who is invited to tell their story. As expected, those invited to testify are those deemed most likely to tell stories supporting the agenda of whomever asked them to participate.

Additionally, some people—such as those categorized as "mentally ill" or as suffering from dementia—can be prevented from storytelling in policy hearings because of cultural codes marking them as unable to tell truthful stories. Exclusions of particular storytellers also can be based on "expert" knowledge. Consider the instance of Vietnam war veterans who were disqualified as witnesses in policy deliberations about increasing public resources for veterans suffering the effects of war trauma. These veterans were disqualified from offering testimony because it was assumed they were unable to tell true stories because of this trauma (Ewick and Silbey 1995). Reflect upon the irony: The policy debate was the result of social movement activists who convinced the public that veterans suffering horribly from their war experiences needed more social resources. Characteristics of the categorical story character—a horribly suffering veteran—became the justification for disqualifying individual veterans from offering testimony in hearings about their own experiences and needs.

Still further, not all stories told in policy hearings are evaluated by policymakers as believable and important. This was powerfully demonstrated in the Tolen Commission hearings in the United States in 1942, organized to obtain citizen input on President Roosevelt's Executive Order authorizing the military to remove Japanese people (citizens and non-citizens alike) from their homes on the West Coast and place them in internment camps because they were considered a danger to the United States, which was at war with Japan. Many Japanese citizens offering testimony in these hearings told self-stories dramatizing how they were good, loyal Americans. Yet policy makers obviously evaluated the competing "America at War" story featuring its disloyal Japanese character as more believable and important than stories of loyalty told by those who testified. We know that because the commission supported the policy of internment (Petonito 1992).

NARRATIVE, POLICY CONTENT, AND POLICY PROCESS

Stories are a critical component of the policy-making process, an often long and complex progression of formal and informal meetings and hearings that define the problem to be resolved by policy as well as define and justify the proposed resolutions of this problem (Campbell 2002; Fischer 2003; Rochefort and Cobb 1994).

Causal Stories and Policy Content

In the first step in the policy process, called "problem definition," problems of a *general* sort are refined to problems of a *particular* sort requiring particular kinds of resolutions that can be mandated by policy (Stone 1997). The process of problem definition is driven by the need to establish facts: What are the problem's costs (in terms of human suffering or taxpayer expense)? What is the problem's cause? How many of what categories of people is the problem affecting? Answers to these questions are in the forms of storied and non-storied testimony, documents entered into the written record, and interactions among policymakers and between policymakers and those offering testimony. These combine to create a *causal story*.

Causal stories establish cause, blame, and responsibility which simultaneously *justifies* solutions of particular types—policy (Stone 1997; Fischer 2003). Causal stories also contain characters who typically are variations of the victim and villain stock characters of social problem formula stories. Such categorical characters are known as the policy's "target population," the categories of people the policy is designed to help or punish. These characterizations are "normative and evaluative, portraying groups in positive or negative terms through symbolic language, metaphors, and stories" (Schneider and Ingram 1993, 334; also see Schneider and Sidney 2009). Causal stories also can contain heroes, who, at times, are human (such as workers in medicine, education, welfare who will put policy into practice), and at other times are non-human (such as rules, procedures, services established by policy).

As expected, the policy-making process in a complex, heterogeneous, and morally fragmented world most often contains multiple competing stories promoting different images of causes, blame, and responsibility. United States Congressional debate about non-profit tax policy, for example, was a contest between two competing stories. In one, "charities" were organizations that did much good and therefore deserved tax-exempt status. A competing story dramatized a large number of organizations *posing* as charities in order to obtain non-justified tax-exempt status. The meaning of philanthropy in one story is altruism, in the other it is tax evasion; charities heroically help the needy in one story, in the other greedy organizations defraud taxpayers. These two stories justify competing answers to questions about whether or not non-profit organizations should be exempt from paying taxes (Jacobs and Sobieraj 2007).

While causal stories are the end result of all that comprises policy deliberations, policy hearings sometimes include testimonies in storied form told by experts, by people whose lives have been affected by the condition being debated, by those who will be policy targets.

An Illustration: Stories and the Problem of Opioid Addiction

The research of Loren Wilburs (2016) demonstrates the work of stories featuring individual characters in policy hearings. This example is from a two-day hearing in February, 2013 sponsored by the Department of Health and Human Services about the "Impact of Approved Labeling on Chronic Opioid Therapy." The hearing's purpose was to strike a balance between allowing the necessary use of opioids for the management of severe pain and preventing the misuse of opioids leading to addiction. The sole hearing content was personal testimonies which combined to produce two competing causal stories.

By far, the most prominent story would be titled the "Danger of Opioids." This story was jointly created through testimonies of parents with children who died opioid-related deaths. These children had been exemplary people: Terri G. describes her son, Tim, as "always a happy kid. . . . He always was my good boy." Pete J. describes his daughter as a "wonderful young lady." The parents of Daniel P. said he was a "Navy veteran who was every parent's dream." Note that these descriptions are of good people who *did* take opioids yet who can *not* be confused with the morally devalued "drug addict" character. the "Danger of Opioids" story contains a second victim: Family members offering testimony. Terri K says she will "forever grieve the loss of my child;" Patricia M.'s sorrow is "I will never see Adrianne's beautiful face again. I will never hear her giggling laughter, I will never watch as she gets married."

There are three villains in the "Danger of Opioids" story. One is human: The physicians who over-prescribe these drugs. Some of these doctors are pure villain characters, a "drug dealer hiding behind a certificate that indicated he had completed medical school," while others are simply ignorant people who should have known the drugs should be very carefully prescribed. Two other villains are non-human: The pharmaceutical companies that knowingly and intentionally "downplayed the risks and exaggerated the benefits" of opioids to increase sales, and the Food and Drug Administration (FDA) that failed to adequately monitor opioid prescriptions and labelling.

Multiple stories told by individuals who testified in these hearings together produce a causal story, the "Danger of Opioids," which contains a clear moral: Whether caused by pharmaceutical company evil or FDA bureaucratic incompetence or physician evil or ineptitude, opioids are over-prescribed. This story supports policies to make it harder to obtain opioid prescriptions and for prescription labels containing strong warnings about their use.

Although the "Danger of Opioids" story was the most common, these hearings produced a contending story, the "Necessity of Opioids." This story contained only one character, the person who desperately needs relief from "astronomically high" pain. Amy A.'s treatment for metastatic melanoma left her with "horrible peripheral neuropathy and leg pain;" Janet needed high-dose opioids to be "able to function as a hairdresser, wife, and mother of two small children;" without heart drugs and opiates, James was on the "floor crying like a baby in response to his continuous chest pain." Again, these people *do* take opioids yet they *cannot* be confused with the "drug addict" character. On the contrary, these are good people asking only for pain relief. The moral of the "Necessity of Opioids" story is that people can have a very real need for these drugs. The story supports a warning: In the rush to prevent opioid abuse do not forgot the victims of medical problems whose need for the drugs is real and morally acceptable.

NARRATIVE AND POLICY JUSTIFICATION

By forming images of cause, blame, and responsibility, causal stories *justify* policy. They justify *why* policy is needed and what *type* of policy is needed; by aligning policy contents with cultural meanings, stories justify the *appropriateness* of policy.

Stories justify the need for policy. Consider how the following story of a single individual, appearing on *Breitbart News*, becomes a justification for policy stopping "illegal immigration." As a character, Grant R., is obviously a good American, killed by a villain categorized as an "illegal alien," a term dramatizing both illegality and otherness ("alien"). The previous heinous crimes of the villain (being a member of a drug cartel, sexual assault), coupled with the virtue of the victim (a hard worker, a wonderful family member), justifies the need for "enforcing immigration laws" both in terms of money ("illegal immigration costs taxpayers billions and billions of dollars,") and morality ("it's costing us our sons and our daughters, our parents, our loved ones").

> The family of Grant R. is showing a video commemorating their son, murdered in January by an illegal alien free on bond. The video also pleads for the enforcement of immigration laws and unveils a new foundation meant to help Americans harmed by illegal alien crime. "Grant was just my buddy, from the minute he was born. He just brightened everybody: My family, my friends. He was everything," Grant's father, Steve R. says . . . after he and his wife divorced, Grant got a job at the Quick Trip mart in Mesa, Arizona, to help pay the bills. "He did this without question or hesitation. It was just the kid he was," Steve R. says. But everything changed on January 22, 2015. "My son's death was completely preventable," Steve R. says. [The person who murdered Grant R. during a robbery] had been in the country illegally since he was 14 and was a self-proclaimed member of the Sinola drug cartel and the Mexican mafia. He had previously been arrested for sexually assaulting a woman . . . holding her captive for a week. And he was able to plead it down to felony burglary. . . . Illegal immigration costs taxpayers billions and billions of dollars, along with Americans' lives. "The cost to us goes way beyond dollars. It's costing us our sons and our daughters, our parents, our loved ones." (McHugh 2016)

Audiences are encouraged to support policies that will help good American characters. "Kids' Health Insurance Hangs in the Balance and Parents Wonder What's Wrong with Congress" is one such story in the *Washington Post*. This family most certainly is a good American family—the couple is thrifty and married, they are good parents, have plans for the future, hold multiple jobs, and volunteer to help others. Yet they are unable to pay for health insurance. The story of this *one* family justifies the need for policy to reduce health insurance costs for *all* families:

As the parents of two young children who have relied on the government-backed health-care plan, the S.'s are unsure whether they should stretch their finances to put their boys, 3 and 3 months, on a private plan—or have faith that a polarized Congress will work it out."$1,200 for the four of us," Ashlee S., 26, said, estimating the plan's monthly cost from their two-bedroom town-house outside Salt Lake City, where she crafts necklaces as part of the family business. "We can't pay that and save for a mortgage, or save anything at all." . . . The tangible effects of [Congressional] inaction reverberated from the S.'s home to doctors' offices and statehouses across the country. Nine million children use CHIP [Child Health Insurance Program] to help lower their medical costs. . . . The S.'s don't know how they would make ends meet if CHIP goes away. To supplement income from Ashlee S.'s necklaces, Levi S. just took a customer service job that he hopes will lead him down the path to become a software developer. . . . With a background in child development, she volunteers at a hospital to help parents and children with terminal illnesses cope. Many of them could only pay with CHIP. (Samuels 2017)

Stories can justify the *need* for policy, and, by aligning policy with cultural values, stories can justify policy *content* (Fischer 2002; Roe 1994; Smith 2005; Stone 1989). That is, in a democracy, policy makers *cannot* say "I voted for this policy because I was paid a lot of money to do so," or "I voted for this policy because I'm prejudiced against the people it will hurt." In this way, "culture makes a difference even if you believe 'interests' are a driving force. . . . Even the most instrumental leaders must legitimate their activities by rhetorical means" (Smith 2005, 49). At least on the record and in public proclamations, policy justifications must align policy content with cultural meanings as these are perceived to be understood by relevant population segments (such as the "American people," or "voters in my district").

An Illustration: The Storied Justification of War

War offers an example of how stories can justify the need for policies of particular types. After all,

Wars involve real threat statements from real leaders, involve real armies and real bombs and real deaths. Yet these brute facts cannot tell us what threats mean or what we should do. They do not tell us whether we should fight or flee or negotiate or impose sanctions or look for diplomatic solutions. (Smith 2005, 29)

Because leaders in democracies cannot simply declare war, they must manufacture cognitive, emotional, and moral consent for the use of force (Clément et al. 2017). For this reason, presidents and prime ministers deploy a war rhetoric that justifies the practicality and morality of war while encouraging emotional reactions supporting war such as national pride, patriotism, fear of the enemy, and sympathy for in-group war casualties (Bostdorff 2003; Coles

2002; Murphy 2003; Smith 2005). Predictably, war rhetoric typically is in story form. "Justifying war" a formula story. In the melodramatic genre, this story features pure victims, evil villains, and saintly heroes in an intense plot of struggle between good and evil (Anker 2005; Johnson 2002; Merskin 2004).

Throughout the day on September 11, 2001, televisions and computer monitors in the United States constantly replayed images of burning, collapsing buildings, people jumping to certain death, chaos on the streets of New York City. Although it *was* clear that these were *not* images from a fictional disaster movie, the meaning of the images was *not* clear. What story did these horrific images tell? What was happening and what should be done in response? The internationally televised 592-word speech of American President George W. Bush, on the evening of September 11, constructed the meanings of the images in the form of a story with a moral that the something that must be done was a "war on terror." The speech begins:

> Good evening. Today, our fellow citizens, our way of life, our very freedom came under attack in a series of deliberate and deadly terrorist acts. The victims were in airplanes, or in their offices; secretaries, businessmen and women, military and federal workers; moms and dads, friends and neighbors. Thousands of lives were suddenly ended by evil, despicable acts of terror. The pictures of airplanes flying into buildings, fires burning, huge structures collapsing, have filled us with disbelief, terrible sadness, and a quiet, unyielding anger. These acts of mass murder were intended to frighten our nation into chaos and retreat. But they have failed; our country is strong. A great people has been moved to defend a great nation.

The speech ends:

> America and our friends and allies join with all those who want peace and security in the world, and we stand together to win the war against terrorism. Tonight, I ask for your prayers for all those who grieve, for the children whose worlds have been shattered, for all whose sense of safety and security has been threatened. And I pray they will be comforted by a power greater than any of us, spoken through the ages in Psalm 23: "Even though I walk through the valley of the shadow of death, I fear no evil, for You are with me." This is a day when all Americans from every walk of life unite in our resolve for justice and peace. America has stood down enemies before, and we will do so this time. None of us will ever forget this day. Yet, we go forward to defend freedom and all that is good and just in our world. Thank you. Good night, and God bless America.

Observers have evaluated this as *not* a good speech when measured by traditional standards because it contained neither memorable rhetoric nor a logic for waging war; its imagery was so simple, it was simplistic (Bostdorff 2003; Murphy 2003). Yet this bad speech was a persuasive melodramatic story:

There was no significant domestic criticism of its contents (Bostdorff 2003), mass media merely echoed his words (Schubert et al. 2002; Entman 2003), and there was overwhelming bipartisan support for the policy—a War on Terror—this speech and those following it advocated (Gaines 2002; Huddy et al. 2002).

The plot of the "Story of September 11" is one of unquestionable horror, of "airplanes flying into buildings, fires burning, huge structures collapsing." The victims are good Americans: They are workers: "secretaries, business-men and women, military and Federal workers," and they are caring people who are "moms and dads, friends." These center stage victims are joined by all Americans who, while not suffering physical harm, feel their "sense of safety and security has been threatened." The villain character, called a ter-rorist, is as bad as the victim is good. The terrorist is pure evil and represents the "very worst of human nature." The horror of the incident, coupled with the less-than-human character of the terrorist implicitly answers the question, why war? Bluntly stated, there can be no "diplomacy" or "negotiation" with evil.

A story of war requires another character: The hero. On the evening of September 11 the good Americans victims were promised that they were destined to be heroes who would "unite in our resolve for justice and peace," who would "find those responsible and bring them to justice," who would "win the war against terrorism."

Seventeen years later, the "Story of September 11" continues to enjoy widespread support from large segments of the American audience. It is a good story because it appeals to a variety of emotions; because it does *not* include contentious meanings such as those surrounding race, class, sexual-ity; and because its powerful melodramatic imagery is perfect for media which has never tired of relaying it.

While it would be absurd to blame a story for what has happened around the world as a consequence of the American-led war on terror, it likewise seems foolish to ignore how wars must be made meaningful to citizens in democracies (Moerk and Pincus 2000). Because meaning is conferred through narrative, narrative is central to creating and maintaining the pos-sibilities of war (Smith 2005).

An Illustration: The American Dream Story and Welfare Reform

Cultural codes surrounding social welfare programs are complex, interlock-ing sets of assumptions including what is normal in relation to employment; the nature, obligations, and rights of citizenship; relationships between social services and family; cultural bases of resource redistribution, and moral val-ues associated with poverty (Pfau-Effinger 2005). Policy determining aid to poor people was massively transformed in the United States in 1996 when the Responsibility and Work Opportunity Reconciliation Act (PRWORA) replaced the many programs associated with Aid to Families with Dependent Children (AFDC) with the Temporary Assistance to Needy Families (TANF) program. The bill was enormously popular among a large majority of tax-paying citizens who believed that the then-current system discouraged both work and marriage while encouraging births to unmarried women, particularly to unmarried minority women. While the bill was identified with Republicans, more Democrats voted for it than against it and Democratic President Clinton signed the bill into law and later touted welfare reform as one of the major accomplishments of his administration.

While enjoying popular support, this legislation made life more difficult for people needing help. It did so by placing limits on lifetime eligibility for benefits; by mandating employment or job training for everyone, including women with small children; by forcing women seeking support to identify the fathers of their children, and by prohibiting teenage mothers from setting up independent households (for analysis of this policy and hearings leading to it, see Graebner 2002; Gring-Pemble 2001; Guetzkow 2010; Hancock 2004; O'Connor 2001; Stryker and Wald 2009).

Several analyses of the dozens of policy hearings leading to this legislation agree there were two contending causal stories featuring diametrically opposed images of the target population for welfare reform, a character most commonly called the "welfare mother." One such causal story features a good American character not responsible for her failure to achieve self-sufficiency; the other features a character who is dependent because of her bad attitudes, bad choices, bad behaviors (Gring-Pemble 2001). Within cultural logic, these two contending stories promote very different cognitive, emotional, and moral orientations toward those requiring assistance, and these support different policy responses: More benefits and fewer burdens for those evaluated as not responsible for needing help; fewer benefits and more burdens for those evaluated as responsible for needing help.

Given the American history of ideas about, and actions toward, poverty and programs of social welfare, it is expectable that the prevailing causal story in the hearings leading to the 1996 welfare reform dramatized welfare recipients as women responsible for their need. Such a character, of course, justifies the punitive policy being passed. Yet, simultaneously, this character is not useful for justifying the morality of punitive policy because policy must be justified *symbolically* in terms of underlying *moral* systems (Lakoff 1996; Stryker and Wold 2009).

The final policy hearing (U.S. House of Representatives, July 31, 1996) contained such justifications for policy changes. This was not a "hearing" in the typical sense because the votes were tallied before it started and all participants knew the bill would pass and the President would sign it. In form, this hearing featured a progression of Representatives, each given a minute or two to justify their support or opposition to the bill. Remarkably, whether Republican *or* Democrat, whether in support *or* in opposition, most speakers formed their justifications in terms of how the bill would—or would not—encourage welfare recipients to *achieve the American dream.*

Testimony produced the scene requiring welfare reform: There was no choice but to reform welfare policy because "we all agree the welfare system does not work," because the current system "undermines the American values of work, opportunity, responsibility, and family . . . the common ideals of the dignity of work and the enduring strength of families." According to one Representative:

> I cannot imagine a policy that is crueler to children than the current welfare system. In the name of compassion, we have unleashed an unmitigated disaster upon America. . . . It penalizes work and learning. It poisons our communities and our country with generation after generation of welfare dependency. It robs human beings of hope and life and any opportunities at the American Dream.
> —United States House of Representatives (1996, H9419–9420)

If the then-current welfare system was immoral because it *violated* American values, it followed that reform must *support* "fundamental American values," explicitly specified as those "moving people toward work and independence," as promoting "work and individual responsibility," as "[s]trengthening families and instilling personal responsibility."

The plot of the American Dream story dramatizing opportunity and success depends upon a particular narrative character, a person with a specific constellation of attitudes and behaviors necessary to take advantage of opportunities assumed to be plentiful. This is the type of person legislators *wanted* welfare policy to promote: They talked about the need for people to be "productive" and "self-reliant," to produce children who will "take their place as productive members of our society." Legislators who complained that the proposed new system was mean-spirited would nonetheless implicitly agree with these preferences by arguing that welfare recipients *already* were women who "want to work," who "want to teach their kids how to take responsibility," who hate welfare and are "desperately trying to escape it."

Not all people then using welfare were evaluated as so morally worthy of assistance. While legislators *never* used the terms of "undeserving" or "unworthy," they made numerous implicit comparisons that authored a deficient welfare recipient character who did not deserve assistance. For example, they talked about the importance of helping those who "*through no fault of their own* must turn to their Government for help in times of need," implying that those requiring help "through fault" did not deserve assistance. They argued governments "should help those *who are too sick, too old or too young to help themselves*," implying the need of those who were not too sick, not too old, or not too young could be ignored. And, they repeatedly praised the proposed legislation for offering a real sense of hope to the *truly needy*, which implicitly applauds the ability of the new legislation to *not* help the "untruly" needy (all emphases added). In brief, those supporting *and* those opposing the legislation drew upon cultural meaning systems supporting the value of independence with accompanying proscriptions against offering resources to those evaluated as failing to help themselves. In that way, the story of the American Dream was a system of meaning organizing *all* testimony: Welfare had to change because it blocked poor people's opportunities to "ever have a chance at the American dream." The new policy was about "providing an American dream for more Americans," it was about liberating families "from welfare dependency and get them working and a chance at the American dream."

Objectively speaking, by reducing benefits and increasing burdens, the 1996 welfare reform made life more difficult for those relying on welfare. Yet *on the record*, the justification for this policy was positive and uplifting, it was about how policy would help poor people achieve the promise of the American Dream. This story obtains power through incorporating widely held and deeply embraced systems of meaning; it also acquires power through making *invisible* multiple inconvenient facts of life in a racist, sexist, capitalist social order. Policy justifications in effect both made racial and gendered hierarchies invisible while institutionalizing those hierarchies (Gordon 1994; Neubeck and Cazenave 2001; Quadagno 1994).

In conclusion, regardless of how policy is motivated and shaped by institutionalized power and material interests, policy must be justified as both instrumentally and morally necessary (Jasper 1992). Because cultural meanings are best conveyed through the narrative form, policy justifications often are in the form of stories. The meaning-making work of stories is woven throughout the process and content of social policy which produces *material* consequences: Policy can add, modify, or delete laws and procedures; it can demand new ways of acting. Policy also can result in social interventions designed to do something about individuals in the categories of people targeted for policy interventions.

STORIES, SOCIAL MOVEMENTS/SOCIAL POLICIES, SOCIAL SERVICES

A common feature of the American social landscape are organizations, programs, and groups designed to do something to help, rehabilitate, or punish those in particular identity categories defined by social movements and/or within social policy. These places range from prisons and mental hospitals to support groups of all types, from shelters for homeless people or abused women to programs for pregnant teens or for children at risk. Some of these places are formally organized with highly trained staff, others are quite informal with untrained, volunteer workers. Despite many differences, these places share a great deal in that each is a consequence of successful creation of social problem consciousness. After all, there would not be rape crisis hotlines without the social problem of rape, prisons exist because of worry about crime, and so on. Also, despite differences, each of these places is organized for people in particular identity categories and offer these *types* of people the *types* of services deemed necessary. What else these places share is that images of clients' characteristics, problems, and needs are organizationally packaged in the form of stories that often are relatively similar to those authored by social movements/social policy,

It is logical that places seeking to intervene in the lives of people defined as troubled would be organized around stories. As noted by Michael Lipsky (1980, 152):

> One cannot practice without an implicit model of the people on whom one is practicing. An open classroom demands a conception of children as requiring relatively greater freedom and flexibility than are available in a traditional classroom. A psychiatrically oriented drug center is founded on a different model of human motivation than a center organized around peer interaction and self-help.

There are multiple ways in which stories influence the actual practice of social service provision. Stories embedded in social policy, for example, can define the parameters of who might *receive* services. Schools receiving money from Title 1 legislation were required to classify individual students in terms of their deficiencies as defined in the legislation leading to these programs (Stein 2001); workers in programs receiving money from "Work Incentive Program" (WIN) legislation were required to classify their clients into a small number of categories predetermined by the legislation (Miller 1991).

Stories embedded in social movements/social policy also can become institutionalized in the form of *client expectations*. For example, successful advocacy on behalf of women victims (abused women, victims of rape or sexual harassment) led to a series of changes in both laws and court procedures designed to make it easier for such women to use court resources. Yet women find that in order to receive court resources they must tell a self-story that workers evaluate as an instance of the "woman-as-pure-victim" story promoted by social problem formula stories as well as embedded in policy (Dunn 2001, 2002; Emerson 1997; Loseke 1992, 2001). In the same way, court-mandated drug treatment programs will not release a client from court monitoring until the "right" story is told (Nolan 2002), prison counselors require that the right story be told, and be told convincingly, before parole is possible (Fox 1999). In all such instances, clients *must* tell self-stories that can be evaluated by organizational workers as versions of the stories leading the programs or organizations.

Stories informing social movements/social policy also can shape organizational *services*. Welfare workers' understandings of the story of "substance-using clients," for example, legitimize particular practices toward these clients (Selseng 2017). Similarly, programs for gay and lesbian youth began with social problem advocacy advancing the argument that such youth required services because they were at risk for emotional, social, and psychological problems, so ensuing programs focus on those problems (Mayberry 2006).

Finally, it is common for the self-stories told by clients to be defined as part of the problem to be resolved. Encouraging clients to change their self-stories to more closely conform to organizationally-sponsored stories is the work of self-help groups of all types who encourage their members to identify as a particular type of story character be it the "gambler" (Rossol 2001), "battering man" (McKendy 1992), "diabetic" (Maines 1991), "transgendered" (Mason-Schrock 1996), "substance using client" (Selseng 2017), "addict" (Anderson 2015), or "Latino" (Santiago-Irizarry 2001).

An Illustration: Social Service Shaping of Client's Self-Stories

Social service workers can attempt to shape clients' stories in ways allowing them to be formally eligible for services such as housing for homeless people (Marvasti 2002; Smith and Anderson 2018) or court protection for women victims of domestic violence (Emerson 1997; Trinch and Berk-Seligson 2002). Nowhere is the molding of stories more obvious than in support groups where it is the goal of facilitators to re-shape the self-stories of group members to those *a priori* defined as better than the stories leading people into the group. The following examples are taken from support groups for women victims of violence (see Loseke 2001 for details on these groups and for further examples).

Because membership in these support groups tend to be very transient, each session starts with a facilitator asking those present to "tell us a little about yourself and why you're here." While commonsense leads most women to interpret this as a request to talk about the violence they experienced which led them to the group, from time to time, women do not tell such an expectable story. Megan, a new group member, responded to the request with the following:

> I'm Megan. I got my divorce, I have my boys. We're living in [another county] and things are really going good. I'm on probation because of him but I'm dealing with it. I beat up his girlfriend and slashed the tires on her car—and I'd do it again if I had to do it all over [laughing]. . . . I still don't know why he left

me for her. He had everything. I worked, he never did. He took off for months at a time on his bike and that was okay. The kids are doing good. They were always used to him being gone a lot anyway. He pays his child support.

In several ways, Megan's story is not relatively consistent with a formula story associated with services for women who are abused: Her story does not include any violence; her character is strong and, indeed, aggressive; her partner is not a good villain because he "pays his child support." Another group member, Jesse, specifically asks Megan to enlarge her story to include the expected violence.

> *Jesse:* Was he physically abusive?

> *Megan:* You name it, he did it. Physically, emotionally, sexually. But I wouldn't have left. In fact, I tried to reconcile for months after he left. I guess I just couldn't handle the fact that I had always done everything for him, supported him, put up with everything he did and he left me for her.

While acknowledging the violence specifically requested, Megan does *not* change her story. Indeed, she further authors the plotline as about the problems of being rejected rather than of being abused. The interaction continues with the facilitator who herself transforms Megan's story into a narrative of abuse when she says, "emotional abuse can certainly be as damaging as physical abuse. Most people don't realize that." The group continues discussing the problems of emotional abuse and does not return to Megan's story of the problems of being rejected.

Some weeks later, another new member, Jane, told her story as follows:

> I'm Jane. I'm just getting out of an abusive relationship with a man I've been living with for four years. I was doing so good. I had a good job until I got laid off two weeks ago. We got a new car because he said he didn't want me driving all the way to the job in the old van. I thought that was good—that he was worried about me. But then when I had to get to work he was out in the new car and I couldn't get to work. I'd been off the booze for four years. I met him at AA. . . . I knew it wasn't going to get any better a couple of weeks ago when I ended up in the emergency room with broken ribs and black eyes. He just came at me and started punching. It was always the same. He starts asking questions and I never have the right answers. . . . Usually, I don't even say anything, it doesn't matter what I say. He doesn't hear what I say. I woke up in the bedroom, I was confused, he told me I'd been drinking, that I got drunk and fell. I couldn't remember. I did start drinking then and didn't stop for a few days, then it started coming back. I remember him hitting me in the kitchen then I must have blacked out . . . and my family was only too ready to believe I was drinking again. They don't want anything to do with me. I screwed up again and they don't want to know about it. So I called here. I'm not crazy but I feel like I'm crazy. Why is this happening to me? It was such a

long battle to stop drinking. I'm an alcoholic but I'm not crazy. Now I'm
babbling again.

Jane's story approaches in form and content what Arthur Frank (1995) calls a
"chaos" narrative: It lacks coherence, the emotions are raw, the pain is over-
determined, and the "impulse of most would-be helpers is first to drag the
teller out of this story" (1995, 111). Jane's story contains multiple plots,
some of which are elements of the formula story of abuse (the violence is
extreme and long lasting, she is a pure victim), other central story themes
include alcohol use, a non-supportive family, and doubts about her sanity. Of
multiple possible themes that could be developed, the facilitator pursues that
of danger, a theme Jane repeatedly resists:

> *Facilitator:* So, he's gone now?
>
> *Jane:* I told him I was going to press charges and he left. He'll be back to get
> his things. I have to find a way to pay the rent, find a job. It'll work out.
>
> *Facilitator:* Do you feel in danger? Do you worry about him coming back?
>
> *Jane:* No, if he comes back, I'll call the police.
>
> *Facilitator:* Do you need help in filing a restraining order?
>
> *Jane:* I don't think I want to do that now. I don't want to think about it now.
>
> *Facilitator:* I'd feel better if you got a restraining order. You know you can
> call the crisis line day or night.

These support group examples demonstrate two important observations
about meaning-making: Self-stories, especially those of people experiencing
trouble, can be confusing, complex, and defy easy understanding; and, while
support-group members and service workers try to change stories not conforming to organizationally preferred stories, people can strongly resist attempts to change their stories, be this the resistance of Megan and Jane
telling self-stories in a support group for women experiencing abuse, boys in
a home for "juvenile delinquents" (Kivett and Warren 2002) or violent men
in prison (Fox 1999). People will refuse to embrace a new story about their
selves and their lives unless the offered story conforms to their own experiences,
their own commonsense understandings, and own their moral evaluations.

NARRATIVE, POLICY, AND SOCIAL STRUCTURE

Stories are central to both the creation and content of social policy, as well as
to the organization of programs and organizations established by policy. The
policy process begins with creating *causal* stories which transform often
vague issues and problems into problems of particular sorts that can be

effectively responded to with policy of particular sorts (Stone 1997); stories align policy contents with the cultural values of dominant population segments which forms the necessary rhetorical justifications of policy (Smith 2005); stories shape social service organization and service provision.

This work of stories in social policy has powerful symbolic and material consequences because it serves to categorize people into two groups: those who are, and those who are not, included in policy target populations. This constructs *symbolic* boundaries around categories of people. When these boundaries are objectified by the rules, regulations, resources, or constraints stemming from policy they create *material* consequences such as unequal access to, and unequal distribution of resources, opportunities, constraints (Lamont and Fournier 1992; Lamont and Molnár 2002; Lamont and Virag 2002). Because categories of people evaluated as morally good receive policy benefits while categories of people constructed as not morally good receive policy burdens (Schneider and Ingram 1993), story characters can be implicated in structuring the "generic processes that produce and perpetuate social inequality" (Kusow and Eno 2015, 409). Stories justify social inequality (Alexander 1992).

Chapter Six

Reflections on Narrative Productions of Meaning in a "Post-Fact" World

My project has been to explore narrative productions of meaning in an era where meaning is a problem created by rapid change, heterogeneity, size, complexity, moral fragmentation, and loss of faith in authorities and institutions previously believed worthy and capable of defining truth. This era is "unsettled" (Swidler 1986) in that many previously accepted ways of acting, thinking, and feeling have been rejected, while profound disagreements have led to what can seem a virtual impossibility of establishing their replacements. It is reasonable to call this a "post-fact" world, where truth has been relativized, where "likes" and "shares" and "bots" instantaneously and endlessly transmit news and fake news, facts and alternative facts, information and misinformation; where immense inequalities lead social members to have vastly different experiences, opportunities, and understandings of how the world does work and how the world should work; where social media partitions particular categories of people into distinct populations whose personal views are continually reinforced by algorithms determining what they will know about the world—and what they will not know. All of this is deeply disturbing within a democratic political order necessarily resting upon perceived common interests, dialogue, debate, and compromise.

My principal argument is that, within such environments, the narrative form has particularly strong meaning-making powers on all stages of social life. Stories are pervasive in both private and public lives because they contextualize events and characters which creates meaning in a chaotic world of constant change and disagreement. Stories are pervasive because they can appeal to emotions in a world where what is felt can seem more real and more important than what is thought. Stories are pervasive because they can speak to questions about morality that are so central to human existence yet so ignored by experts of all types.

THEMES IN SOCIAL SCIENCE PERSPECTIVES ON NARRATIVE PRODUCTIONS OF MEANING

While literary critics, film critics, and religious scholars have long histories of interest in narratives, my perspective as a social observer leads me to be more interested in stories told as fact rather than as fiction, fantasy, fairy tale, or myth; more interested in stories containing characters who are human rather than mythical, animal, or cartoon; more interested in stories circulating in social life rather than residing in libraries or kindles; and more interested in what stories *do* in social life rather than their universal, formal, or structural properties. Four themes have woven their ways through my discussion: Narratives are social in their contents, meanings, evaluations, and consequences; narrative meaning is cognitive, emotional, and moral; narrative meaning has personal, interactional, and cultural dimensions; and narrative is a tool of power.

Narratives are Social in their Contents, Meanings, Evaluations, and Consequences

The first theme organizes all others: Everything about narrative is social. Narratives are social in their *contents* and *meanings* because the raw material for stories are socially circulating cultural codes, which are systems of ideas reflecting common ways of thinking and feeling. Narratives are social in their *evaluations* because audience members use their own experiences, understandings of cultural codes, common sense, and moral sensibilities to evaluate story believability and importance. Stories are social in their *consequences* because they do things in the social world.

Narrative Meaning is Cognitive, Emotional, and Moral; Narrative Meaning has Cultural, Interactional, and Personal Dimensions

My second theme is that narrative meaning is cognitive, emotional, and moral; and the third theme is that narrative meaning has cultural, interactional, and personal dimensions. I am combining these characteristics because together they offer a straightforward answer to a fundamental question of why narrative is so important on all stages of social life: Stories are pervasive because they can speak to thinking *and* feeling *and* moral evaluation *and* they do this on all stages of social life from the most social psychological—the stories we tell ourselves—to the most geopolitical—stories circulating on the world stage.

Narrative is a Tool of Power

Although my orienting questions are about narrative as a method of mean-ing-making, such questions about *subjectivity* straightforwardly uncovered *material* consequences of meaning construction and these consequences have political dimensions. Stories justify social hierarchy and unequal treatment of those in particular categories of actors; stories persuade publics to condemn some—and only some—conditions creating suffering so they justify offering public symbolic and material resources to alleviate some—and only some—conditions; stories are a central organizing device of policy and policy hear-ings which establish laws, procedures, and services that make life easier for people in some—and only some—categories and more difficult for people in other categories. Meaning justifies power. Under the institutionalized forms of power most often of interest to social observers lies the meaning-making power of narrative.

IMPLICATIONS FOR STUDYING NARRATIVE PRODUCTIONS OF MEANING

Until the 1980s, academics shunned narratives which were berated as an "ambiguous, particularistic, idiosyncratic, and imprecise way of representing the world" (Ewick and Silbey 1995, 198), and therefore not worthy of schol-arly attention. In stark contrast, narrative now is a topic of significant interest in a wide variety of disciplines and professional specialties. This journey through the theoretical and empirical literature leads to four insights impor-tant for advancing narrative theory and research.

Exploring Narrative Meaning Requires Multidisciplinary Theory and Methods

Narrative meaning-making takes place on all private and public stages of social life. In consequence, narrative is *simultaneously* about the personal, the social, and the cultural, and about private life as well as about public social processes, social forces, and social institutions. It follows that fully understanding how stories work and the work stories do requires using theo-retical and methodological tools associated with several social science disci-plines (including sociology, political science, communication, public policy, psychology, anthropology, gender studies, international studies) as well as insights from several professions (particularly medicine, social work, educa-tion, and law). Unfortunately, this does not describe the current situation where most literature is separated into disciplines: Sociologists publish in journals read primarily by sociologists, communication scholars publish pri-marily in journals read by other communication scholars; similar concepts go by different names in different disciplines, and so on. Such disciplinary divides inhibit fully understanding the work of stories in social life.

Exploring Narrative Meaning Requires Bridging "Micro-Meso-Macro" Divides

The academic literature also reflects micro, meso, and macro segregations within disciplines. So, theory and empirical work attending to social-psychological questions about how individuals shape self-stories often does little to place those stories into the historical, social, and political contexts of their creation or evaluation (Atkinson and Delamont 2006; Clough 2000; Gubrium and Holstein 2002); research about how stories encourage social problem consciousness rarely asks about the ways in which those same stories do—or do not—help individuals craft adequate self stories or how these stories shape social policy or social service provision. Such divides within disciplines inhibit understanding how narrative works across cultural, institutional, organizational, interactional, and psychological realms of social life.

Exploring Narrative Meaning Requires Attending to the Production, Content, and Consequences of Meaning

There are three questions about narrative meaning: *How* a story produces meaning, *what* meaning a story produces, and the *consequences* of meaning produced by a story. While Jaber Gubrium and James Holstein (Gubrium and Holstein 1997; Holstein and Gubrium 2000) offer an excellent theoretical framework as well as sound practical advice for examining the "what" and "how" questions, studies focusing tightly on the processes of meaning creation often do not continue exploring the *consequences* of this meaning. This allows the practical and political consequences of narrative meaning to remain in a largely unexamined background.

Exploring Narrative Meaning Requires Suspending Interest in an Empirical Truth

Within a world characterized by dramatic differences among social members in their characteristics, opportunities, and experiences, it should be expected that there often are sharp differences between scientifically generated *empirical* truth and audience evaluated *story* truth which reflects the world as cognitively, emotionally, and morally experienced (Gubrium and Holstein 2009; Hoffmaster 2014; Holstein and Gubrium 2012: Loseke 2012, 2018). I would argue that given such predictability, differences between empirical and story truths deserve little more than notice and mention. What must be fully explored are the ways in which particular stories do—or do not—

achieve story truth as evaluated by particular audiences encountering particular stories told for particular reasons on particular occasions.

That said, it nonethess is important to not lose sight of the critical *consequences* of what seems to be the increased importance of story truth. In a not-so-distant past, story truth and empirical truth existed simultaneously and competed with one another. Now, an anti-science, anti-fact social climate characterized by distrust and moral fragmentation is reducing belief in empirical truth for significant portions of the population. This leads story truth to be the only truth. When unmoored from concern with matters of fact beyond those of individual experience and individual belief, this is *dangerous*. As such, it is yet another reason why it is important to understand narrative productions of meaning.

IMPLICATIONS FOR SOCIAL ACTIVISM AND SOCIAL CHANGE

This tour through narrative productions of meaning uncovered insights with implications for both understanding and encouraging social change.

Story Believability Cannot be Effectively Challenged by "Facts"

Detailing the ways in which a story fails to accurately convey an empirical reality is *not* the best route to convincing audiences to evaluate a story as unbelievable. This makes sense in a commonsense sort of a way: Empirical truth can be a statistical abstraction not necessarily reflecting practical experiences; empirical truth can seem to be without emotion or insensitive to moral sensibilities. As such, empirical truth can seem not especially important until it relatively conforms to truth as grounded in practical experiences, commonsense, and judgments of morality. Indeed, challenging a story by emphasizing the ways in which it fails to conform to empirical truth can be *counterproductive* because audience members actively resist criticisms taken to imply their experiential, emotional, or moral realities are *wrong* (Barcelos and Gubrium 2014; Cohen 1997; Ferrence 2012; Fisher 1984; Kirkman et al. 2001; Seccombe et al. 1998). Only stories can effectively challenge other stories.

Stories can Encourage Emotional Responses; Emotional Responses can Encourage Practical Actions

An enduring question about relationships in a world of strangers is when and how audiences feel compassion for unknown others who are suffering (Boltanski 1999; Höijer 2004; Huiberts and Joye 2018; Ong 2014). While the primary empirical concern has been with *media* created images of *extreme* suffering of people in *far away* places, the theoretical issue is far larger:

Images that might encourage emotional responses have a variety of authors; there are multiple degrees and varieties of suffering; others who are suffering might be strangers but not all that far away.

In a commencement speech in 2006, President Barack Obama argued that considerable talk about the "federal deficit" was disguising another deficit in the United States

> I think we should talk more about our empathy deficit—the ability to put ourselves in someone else's shoes; to see the world through those who are different from us—the child who's hungry, the laid-off steelworker, the immigrant woman cleaning your dorm room. (Obama 2006)

Since 2006, the empathy deficit has not been reduced. Indeed, a range of social conditions and social forces—from media fragmentation to increasing inequalities—continually feed the inability to understand the experiences, world views, choices, constraints, and opportunities of others—be those refugees at the southern border or starving children in Yemen. Further, while concern typically is with how publics can be encouraged to feel emotions such as empathy/sympathy/compassion for those who are suffering, just as important are questions about the emotions of anger/hatred/fear directed toward unknown others such as "illegal immigrants," "terrorists," or, at times in the United States, "welfare mothers." What ties all of this together is that emotions are *social* in their origins which means they can be shaped, they can be encouraged—or discouraged (Clark 1997; Shott 1979, Ruiz-Junco 2017). Encouraging audiences to feel in particular ways is the work of stories. Stories—not research, not appeals to logic—are the route to mobilizing emotion (Slovic 2007; Small et al. 2006).

Stories Can Support Institutionalized Power Even When Seeming to Resist This Power

Observers can be quite optimistic about the positive potentials of stories to offer less stigmatized images of socially devalued identities (Plummer 1995) and to encourage social activism leading to positive social change (Davis 2002). While this is a *potential*, stories do not necessarily support social justice. Indeed, because widely circulating stories are "likely to bear the marks of existing social inequalities, disparities of power, and ideological effects" (Ewick and Silbey 1995, 222), stories often support, rather than challenge, existing structures of power and inequality. Clearly, the "good American" character pervasive in stories on all stages of social life reflects and perpetuates models of behavior, attitudes, and motivations required by a society organized around individualistic capitalism. As well, the morally pure victim character reflects and perpetuates a society where sympathy and help are offered only to those evaluated as "morally worthy" with moral worthiness a system of ideas capable of disguising underlying assumptions about race, class, gender, citizenship, and so on. Additionally, story contents dramatizing the extreme harm experienced by victim characters encourage audiences to ignore prevention as well as harm evaluated as less than devastating.

Further, stories that *do* support social change all but invariably focus on individuals rather than on social structure. Consider, for example, the implications of social problems formula stories which tend to be character-driven and featuring one-dimensional victim and villain characters. When encompassed within public moral arguments, such stories can be persuasive in convincing audiences to define harmful conditions as intolerable which, in turn, can lead to both subjective and material changes. Yet such stories both reflect and perpetuate the cultural code of *individualism*: Story scenes typically are undeveloped which means social structures, social forces, and social institutions creating the harm are all but invisible. As such, stories support solutions to help victims rather than to change social structure. In this way, the narrative turn in the social sciences can be understood as a reflection of the *personalization of culture* (Atkinson and Delamont 2006) supporting a therapeutic society organized around adjusting individuals rather than structural change (Furedi 2004).

A specific case in point is the story of gay and lesbian youth as troubled people struggling with their socially stigmatized identity. While this story has been relatively effective in justifying programs and services for such youth, it conveys an image that other than heterosexuality is a *personal* problem (Quinlivan 2002). What this story does *not* do is dramatize how any problems experienced by these youth are created by the social environment as well as how social activism—rather than social services—can be empowering (Mayberry 2006).

Stories Migrating from One Realm to Another Can Have Unintended Consequences

Stories are authored for particular purposes and these shape story characteristics. For example, socially circulating stories that are useful for creating self-stories are complex, multidimensional, and capable of making sense of the contradictions and change that define practical experience. Conversely, stories useful to social activists contain one-dimensional characters, as well as morally unambiguous plots and morals because these characteristics best persuade audiences to define a condition as intolerable. Yet it is common for stories to migrate from one realm to another and, in such cases, characteristics that make a story excellent for accomplishing some tasks can make it a less than adequate resource for accomplishing others.

A general case in point are relationships between the victim character in social problems formula stories and the kinds of stories required in legal proceedings stemming from victimization. The characteristics of social problem formula stories can be a "necessary element of a communication strategy to improve the position of victims," yet such stories can "impose a normative demand upon victims" whose self-stories must be evaluated as relatively conforming to the social movement story if they "wish to receive a sympathetic reaction to their ordeal" (Pemberton et al. 2018, 13).

A specific example is the "woman as victim" narrative such as social problem formula stories of intimate partner violence, sexual harassment, and rape. As tools of social change, these stories have been relatively effective in changing aspects of the *symbolic* world: Women's stories of victimization are not as silenced as in the not-so-distant past; violence against women is less likely than in the past to be treated in a humorous way. Women as victim narratives also have been relatively effective in changing the *material* world: There now are laws, programs and services to help victims and to punish villains. However, there have been unintended consequences when stories authored to encourage social problem consciousness migrate to the realm of social services: Simply stated, social problem formula stories have become a standard by which to evaluate individual women seeking assistance (Mildorf 2002; Schuller and Vidmar 1992). In consequence, women victims of sexual harassment (Dunn 2001) and abuse (Rothenberg 2002, 2003) can find their unique stories and selves evaluated by physicians, police, court workers, or social service providers as not meeting the melodramatic image of extreme harm and absolute moral purity contained in the formula story. Women are taken seriously only when their characteristics and experiences can be evaluated as relatively similar to the story leading social change.

NARRATIVE AND POLITICAL PROCESSES

Although the Enlightenment era privileged the importance of logic in leading democratic debate, citizens always have made political decisions on the basis of logic *and* emotion *and* moral evaluations (Westin 2007; Marcus 2000, 2002). As such, stories are central to the democratic process.

This centrality of stories is distressing given the characteristics of stories and their circulation in the current era. In a not-so-distant past, stories tended to have authors who were named and either personally known or identified as experts or institutional representatives who could be trusted to tell stories that were true. In contrast, anyone now can write stories, authors can be anonymous or deliberately misrepresent their social and political positions. Stories in a not-so-distant past also could achieve widespread circulation only through media confined to network television, radio, newspapers, and magazines that were regulated and, by current standards, remarkably slow. In contrast, stories now can be globally and instantaneously transmitted; transmission routes are connected in ways that are unknowable, constantly changing, and not regulated. Despite this, stories nonetheless are at the core of democratic processes.

Citizen Knowledge and Narrative

Democracies require informed citizens. Because it is not possible for citizens to have independent knowledge of the countless and ever changing conditions requiring public attention, media of all types become the conveyers of information about the world outside practical experience. According to Philip Smith, media are the new public sphere, the "ideas forum and narrative engine of our time" (Smith 2005, 51). Understanding the processes of democracy therefore requires understanding the ways in which media construct stories. I will use one example to demonstrate what all people know from practical experience: Media produced stories can be so different that they promote exceedingly dissimilar cognitive, emotional, and moral orientations toward public issues.

As I write this at the end of 2018, one of the many topics of current political debate is immigration, particularly that of migrants from politically unstable, violence-torn, poverty stricken Central American countries. In the early fall of 2018 attention was focused on a "migrant caravan," a quite large group of migrants who had walked to the United States in order to seek asylum. Multiple visions of realities lie behind that scant, agreed upon description. Is this group primarily composed of families or of lone young men? Are they seeking safety from violence or a life of leisure living off United States welfare? The answers to such questions shape the foundational issue for social policy: Should these migrants be treated compassionately (offered asylum and assistance) or harshly (deported back to their homelands)?

The following two stories appeared on November 23, 2018. Both are about how a portion of the migrant group had made its way to Tijuana, Mexico which is on the boarder of California. The first article is from *Reuters*, an international news agency headquartered in London, England. Focusing on youth in this caravan, the title, "Crime Menaces Migrants on Mexico Boarder as Tijuana Declares Crisis," directs readers to understand these migrants as *victims*. While written by a journalist, this story is told in the voices of the youth, human rights activists, social service providers, and a mayor; understanding these youth as victims is supported by individual stories, warnings that LGBT youth would be specifically targeted for victimization, and reports about the lack of food and shelter. The conclusion of this story is the emotional testimony of one youth who, crying, asked his mother for her blessing before he left his home because his life had been threatened and he did not want to die. This story encourages both the emotion of *com-

passion as well as a evaluation that the American "get tough policies" noted in this story are *not* morally justified.

> Some 4,600 migrants from the bedraggled caravans whose advance has angered U.S. President Donald Trump are camped out with blankets and little food in an overcrowded stadium in Tijuana, whose mayor has declared a "humanitarian crisis." Trump has sent troops to the U.S.-Mexico border, authorized the use of lethal force and threatened to shut down the frontier entirely if the migrant caravans are not stopped. Among the Central Americans, many of whom are Hondurans fleeing violence and poverty in the struggling region, are about 80 minors between the ages of 10 and 17, according to migrants rights groups. Josue, a 15-year-old Honduran in Tijuana, said that during a previous attempt to cross into the United States last year he was kidnapped and badly beaten in Mexico by drug traffickers claiming to be from the notorious Zetas gang. "I ended up in the hospital, I don't know how, because I arrived there half-dead," he said, declining to give his second name. . . . Juan Manuel Gastelum, Tijuana's mayor, said late on Thursday that the city was facing a humanitarian crisis and that supporting the migrants was costing more than 500,000 pesos ($25,000) a day. He urged international agencies to help Tijuana. Activists fear the Central Americans could be stranded for a long time in the city, where some protests against the presence of the caravan have broken out. . . . Stalled for days, migrants from the caravan have been signing onto the waiting list [for process applications for U.S. entry]. They include gay and transgender teenagers. Erika Pinheiro, director of litigation at Al Otro Lado, an immigration legal advocacy group, last week told a Californian court under oath that "LGBT children cannot safely stay in Mexico. They are at risk of violence and persecution." Tijuana has just one shelter for migrant children, which subsists with the help of civic organizations. "Young people are definitely the most vulnerable in this type of movement," said Mynor Contreras, who runs the local YMCA. "We've never received so many in such a short time." If the children cannot enter the United States, they risk being deported from Mexico. That can spell big trouble. "I don't want to die," said 16-year-old Justin, who related how his life was threatened last month for not paying a "war tax" that gangsters charged for his small used-clothing business in the Honduran city of San Pedro Sula. "That day I told my mother to give me her blessing and I left," he said, crying. (Diaz, 2018)

A second story about the migrant caravan was carried by *Fox News*: "Tijuana Declares Humanitarian Crisis as Migrant Group that Split from Caravan Pushes Toward Border." While "humanitarian crisis" *is* in the title, the story contains only one statement (from a migrant leader) about sick children and cold and hungry people. The focus of the story is on the high financial cost of caring for the migrants. What audiences learn about the migrants themselves is that they are demanding, refuse to apply for Mexican humanitarian visas, and refuse to work at readily available jobs. This story encourages an emotion of *anger* as well as morally supports the conclusion that migrants are demanding—not grateful—and have choices so they should be prohibited from entering the United States:

> Tijuana's mayor defiantly slammed his country's federal government for fail-ing to provide adequate aid for the migrant caravan and vowed not to bankrupt his city to care for the thousands now massed near the U.S. border. Mayor Juan Manuel Gastelum . . . called the situation a humanitarian crisis and claimed the Mexican federal government had not helped the city deal with the massive influx of migrants. . . . Meanwhile, a small group of Central American mi-grants marched to a border crossing on Thursday to demand better conditions in shelters housing them. . . . They criticized the conditions at the shelters and said they deserved better. "There are sick children here, and we are cold and hungry," said Carlos Lopez, a Honduran who was leading the group. "The whole world is watching what is happening here." Municipal authorities have acknowledged they are ill-equipped to handle the growing number of migrants arriving in the city. The Arizona Republic reported that the Tijuana municipal government estimated it has spent nearly $27,000 a day to house and care for the migrants. "I will not compromise public services," Gastelum told reporters. "I will not spend Tijuanans' money, I will not bring Tijuana into debt now, in the same way we haven't done so these past two years." Migrants have been urged to apply for humanitarian visas in Mexico and seek work in Tijuana, where officials said there are thousands of jobs available. . . . President Trump demanded Friday that lawmakers on both sides of the aisle come together to tackle border security. "Republicans and Democrats MUST come together, finally, with major Border Security package, which will include funding for the Wall," he wrote. "After 40 years of talk, it is finally time for action. Fix the Border, for once and for all, NOW!" (Suarez Sang 2018)

What citizens "know" about the world beyond practical experience depends upon a media which packages information into stories that can vary widely in terms of their characters, plots, and morals which, in turn, encourage very different orientations to public issues. On one hand, encountering such a blizzard of conflicting meanings might have positive consequences if it en-courages citizens to reflect on the complexity and multidimensionality of issues. Yet that does not always happen because citizens can choose which kinds of stories they wish to encounter and limit themselves to only those stories they find compatible with their existing attitudes, beliefs, and moral evaluations.

Political Platforms and Narrative

Democratic politics, of course, are about political parties and platforms. George Lakoff (1996, 2004, 2009), a cognitive linguist and political philoso-pher, has argued that the Republican party for the past 40 years has effective-ly packaged its policies in ways leading to local, state, and national electoral successes while the Democratic party has failed to do so and has therefore experienced electoral losses. Lakoff's comments (1996, 19) from over 20 years ago remain relevant:

> As long as liberals ignore the moral, mythic, and emotional dimension of politics, as long as they stick to policy and interest groups and issue-by-issue debate, they will have no hope of understanding the nature of the political transformation that has overtaken this country and they will have no hope of changing it.

Policies must be packaged and the most effective package is the narrative form. Robert Reich, who held posts in the Ford, Carter, and Clinton administrations, and who currently is a professor in the School of Public Policy at University of California, Berkeley, summarizes the necessity of packaging platforms and policies into stories:

> [P]eople don't think in terms of isolated policies or issues. If they're to be understandable, policies and issues must fit into larger narratives about where we have been as a nation, what we are up against, and where we should be going. Major shifts in governance—in party alignments and political views—have been precipitated by one party or the other becoming better at telling . . . stories. (2005, 17)

Not all political operatives have understood this as practical advice. Like Lakoff, Reich is critical of those in the Democratic party for what he perceives as their failures:

> [A]lthough Democrats have finally started talking about how they can recast their ideas to best appeal to the public, they've failed to realize that the rhetorical challenge they face is deeper than simply finding the right words and phrases. For Democrats to win back the heart and soul of the electorate, they have to speak to the basic stories that have defined and animated the United States since its founding. (2005, 16)

Reich's contention that electoral success lies in packaging policies and platforms into the "basic stories that have defined and animated the United States" leads me to return one final time to the American Dream, a story called a "force in national consciousness" (Dearin 1997, 699). This particular story is especially pertinent for discussions of political processes because, over the past 100 years, the story has been used in political campaigns to morally justify both conservative *and* progressive agendas (Dearin 1997; Fisher, 1973; Medhurst 2016; Neville-Shepard 2017; Rowland and Jones 2007).

This is possible because, as a story, the American Dream is open to multiple interpretations. The now dominant version that I developed in chapter 2 and have been using throughout this book is the materialistic or individualistic version (Medhurst 2016; Rowland and Jones 2007). This version is

> grounded on the puritan work ethic and relates to the values of effort, persistence, "playing the game," initiative, self-reliance, achievement, and success. It undergirds competition as the way of determining personal worth, the free enterprise system and the notion of freedom, defined as the freedom from controls, regulations, or constraints that hinder the individual's striving for ascendancy in the social-economic hierarchy of society. (Fisher 1973, 161)

Regardless of its current pervasiveness, the materialistic/individualistic version of the Dream story rose to political and social dominance only during the administration of Ronald Reagan in the early 1980s. Previous to that, another version of the story, called moralistic or communal (Medhurst 2016; Rowland and Jones 2007) was more dominant. The moralistic/communal version is

> well expressed in basic tenets of the Declaration of Independence: that "all [people] are created equal," [people] "are endowed by their Creator with certain inalienable rights," among these are "life, liberty and the pursuit of Happiness," governments are instituted to secure these rights. . . . These tenets naturally involve the values of tolerance, charity, compassion, and true regard for the dignity and worth of each and every individual. (Fisher 1973, 161)

Joel Best (2018, 36) argues that sociologists tend to have a "critical, even hostile orientation" toward the ideas in the American Dream and there is considerable evidence that this story is a mere ideological disguise of the myriad ways social class is more fixed than flexible in the United States (Frank 2004; Hochschild 2001; Jackson 2012; Porter 2010). Such complaints are about the materialistic/individualistic version of the story and do not attend seriously to the political potentials of the moralistic/communal version of the story that supported the progressive agendas known as New Deal and New Frontier (Dearin 1997; Medhurst 2016). Robert Rowland and John Jones (2007) note how poll after poll shows that many Americans elect conservative politicians while rejecting conservative policies. They believe this indicates that the conservative ascendance in local, state, and national politics "has not been tied to an ideological victory, but to a narrative victory in which a version of the American Dream privileging individual over communal responsibility has dominated political discourse" (2007, 427). Perhaps the time has come to consider the political potential of the moralistic/communal version of the American Dream.

Here is one such story that opened the keynote address of a young senator from Illinois to the 2004 Democratic National Convention:

Tonight is a particular honor for me because, let's face it, my presence on this stage is pretty unlikely. My father was a foreign student, born and raised in a small village in Kenya. He grew up herding goats. . . . Through hard work and perseverance my father got a scholarship to study in a magical place: America which stood as a beacon of freedom and opportunity to so many who had come before. While studying here, my father met my mother. She was born in a town on the other side of the world, in Kansas. The day after Pearl Harbor he signed up for duty. . . . My parents shared not only an improbable love; they shared an abiding faith in the possibilities of this nation. . . . They imagined me going to the best schools in the land, even though they weren't rich, because in a generous America you don't have to be rich to achieve your potential. . . . And I stand here today, grateful for the diversity of my heritage, aware that my parents' dreams live on in my precious daughters. I stand here knowing that my story is part of the larger American story, that I owe a debt to all of those who came before me, and that, in no other country on earth, is my story even possible.

—Barack Obama

While the people in this story are instances of the hardworking, family centered, morally upright good American character, this story is not about their unrelenting labor, it is not about achieving material success. No, this is a story about the United States as a "magical place" of freedom and opportunity. This is a story supporting hope rather than hate, friendship rather than fear; a story promoting cooperation rather than confrontation, compassion rather than competition, empathy rather than apathy. This is a good story.

* * *

Yes, it would be absurd to argue that the social and political world can be transformed simply by telling different stories. Yes, authoring stories evaluated as believable by a significant number of citizens in a fragmented world is, indeed, challenging. Yes, it is fanciful to believe that the answers to countless problems of identity, social problems, social policy, and social services are found simply in stories told and heard.

Yet it seems just as absurd to dismiss stories because they are, after all, just "stories," or to do little more than criticize differences between story truth and empirical truth. Stories are anything but innocent conveyers of information. Stories produce meanings on all stages of social life. Because these meanings shape both subjective understandings and material realities, understanding the meaning-making work of stories is critical to understanding social life in a world of troubled meaning.

References

Aguirrre, Adalberto, Jr., Edgar Rodriguez, and Jennifer K. Simmers. 2011. "The Cultural Production of Mexican Identity in the United States: An Examination of the Mexican Threat Narrative." *Social Identities* 17: 695–707.

Alcoff, Linda, and Laura Gray. 1993. "Survivor Discourse: Transgression or Recuperation?" *Signs: Journal of Women in Culture and Society* 18: 260–290.

Alexander, Jeffrey C. 1992. "Citizen and Enemy as Symbolic Classification: On the Polarizing Discourse of Civil Society." In *Cultivating Differences: Symbolic Boundaries and the Making of Inequality*, edited by Michèle Lamont and Marcel Fournier, 289–308. Chicago: University of Chicago Press.

Alexander, Jeffrey C. 2010. *The Performance of Politics: Obama's Victory and the Democratic Struggle for Power*. New York: Oxford University Press.

Alexander, Jeffrey C. 2017. *The Drama of Social Life*. Malden, MA: Polity.

Alexander, Jeffrey C., and Jason L. Mast. 2006. "Introduction: Symbolic Interaction and Practice: The Cultural Pragmatics of Symbolic Action." In *Social Performance: Symbolic Action, Cultural Pragmatics, and Ritual*, edited by Jeffrey C. Alexander, Bernhard Giesen, and Jason L. Mast. Cambridge, MA: Cambridge University Press.

Alexander, Jeffrey C., and Philip Smith. 1993. "The Discourse of American Civil Society: A New Proposal for Cultural Studies." *Theory and Society* 22: 151–207.

Alford, C. Fred. 1997. "The Political Psychology of Evil." *Political Psychology* 18: 1–15.

Altheide, David L. 2002. *Creating Fear: News and the Construction of Crisis*. Hawthorne, NY: Aldine deGruyter.

Anderson, Ditte. 2015. "Stories of Change in Drug Treatment: A Narrative Analysis of the 'Whats' and 'Hows' in Institutional Storytelling." *Sociology of Health & Illness* 37: 1–15.

Andrews, M. 2007. *Shaping History: Narratives of Political Change*. Cambridge, UK: Cambridge University Press.

Anker, Elisabeth. 2005. "Villains, Victims and Heroes: Melodrama, Media and September 11." *Journal of Communication* 55: 22–37.

Aristotle. 1926. *The Art of Rhetoric*. Translated by J. H. Freese. Loeb Classical Library 195. Cambridge, MA: Harvard University Press.

Asen, Robert. 2003. "Women, Work, Welfare: A Rhetorical History of Images of Poor Women in Welfare Policy Debates." *Rhetoric & Public Affairs* 6: 285–312.

Atkinson, Paul, and Sara Delamont. 2006. "Rescuing Narrative from Qualitative Research." *Narrative Inquiry* 16: 164–172.

Baker, Phyllis L. 1996. "'Doin' What it Takes to Survive': Battered Women and the Consequences of Compliance to a Cultural Script." *Studies in Symbolic Interaction* 20: 73–98.

Barbalet, Jack. 2002. "Introduction: Why Emotions are Crucial." In *Emotions and Sociology*, edited by Jack Barbalet, 1–9. Cambridge, MA: Blackwell Publishing.

Barcelos, Christie A., and Aline C. Gubrium. 2014. "Reproducing Stories: Strategic Narratives of Teen Pregnancy and Motherhood." *Social Problems* 61: 466–481.

Barnett, Barbara. 2005. "Perfect Mother or Artist of Obscenity? Narrative and Myth in a Qualitative Analysis of Press Coverage of the Andrea Yates Murders." *Journal of Communication Inquiry* 29: 9–29.

Barthes, Roland. 1977. *Image, Music, Text.* New York: Hill & Wang.

Barthes, Roland. 1982. *T.S. Kuhn and Social Science.* London: MacMillan.

Beckwith, Karen. 2014. "Narratives of Defeat: Explaining the Effects of Loss in Social Movements." *The Journal of Politics* 77: 2–13.

Bellah, Robert N., Richard Madsen, William M. Sullivan, Ann Swidler, and Steven M. Tipton. 1985. *Habits of the Heart: Individualism and Commitment in American Life.* Berkeley: University of California Press.

Berbrier, Mitch. 1998. "'Half the Battle': Cultural Resonance, Framing Processes, and Ethnic Affectations in Contemporary White Separatist Rhetoric." *Social Problems* 45: 431–449.

Berbrier, Mitch. 2000. "Ethnicity in the Making: Ethnicity Work, the Ethnicity Industry, and a Constructionist Framework for Research." In *Perspectives on Social Problems*, Volume 12, edited by James A. Holstein and Gale Miller, 69–87. Greenwich, CT: JAI Press.

Berger, Arthur Asa. 1997. *Narratives in Popular Culture, Media, and Everyday Life.* Thousand Oaks, CA: Sage.

Berger, Ronald J., and Richard Quinney. 2005. "The Narrative Turn in Social Inquiry." In *Storytelling Sociology: Narrative as Social Inquiry*, edited by Ronald J. Berger and Richard Quinney, 1–12. Boulder, CO: Lynn Reiner.

Bergstrand, Kelly, and James M. Jasper. 2018. "Villains, Victims, and Heroes in Character Theory and Affect Control Theory." *Social Psychology Quarterly* 81: 228–247.

Berns, Nancy. 2011. *Closure: The Rush to End Grief and What it Costs Us.* Philadelphia: Temple University Press.

Bernstein, Mary. 1997. "Celebration and Suppression: The Strategic Uses of Identity by the Lesbian and Gay Movements." *American Journal of Sociology* 103: 531–565.

Best, Joel. 1997. "Victimization and the Victim Industry." *Society* 34: 9–17.

Best, Joel. 2018. *American Nightmares: Social Problems in an Anxious World.* Oakland: University of California Press.

Bohmer, Carol, and Amy Shuman. 2007. "Producing Epistemologies of Ignorance in the Political Asylum Application Process." *Identities: Global Studies in Culture and Power* 14: 603–629.

Boltanski, Luc. 1999. *Distant Suffering: Morality, Media and Politics.* Cambridge, MA: Cambridge University Press.

Borland, Elizabeth. 2014. "Storytelling, Identity, and Strategy: Perceiving Shifting Obstacles in the Fight for Abortion Rights in Argentina." *Sociological Perspectives* 57: 488–505.

Bostdorff, Denise M. 2003. "George W. Bush's Post-September 11 Rhetoric of Covenant Renewal: Upholding the Faith of the Greatest Generation." *Quarterly Journal of Speech* 89: 293–319.

Bowman, Wayne D. 2006. "Why Narrative? Why Now?" *Research Studies in Music Education* 27: 5–20.

Brands, H. W. 2010. *American Dreams: The United States Since 1945.* New York: Penguin Group.

Brooks, Peter. 1976. *The Melodramatic Imagination: Balzac, Henry James, Melodrama, and the Mode of Excess.* New Haven, CT: Yale University Press.

Brown, Elizabeth A. 2012. "Clean Needles and Bad Blood: Needle Exchange as Morality Policy." *Journal of Sociology and Social Welfare* 39: 121–141.

Bruner, Jerome. 1987. "Life as Narrative." *Social Research* 54: 11–32.

Bruner, Jerome. 2010. "Narrative, Culture, and Mind." In *Telling Stories: Language, Narrative, and Social Life*, edited by Deborah Schiffrin, Anna De Fina, and Anastasia Nylund, 45–50. Washington, DC: Georgetown University Press.

Brush, Paula Stewart. 1999. "The Influence of Social Movements on Articulations of Race and Gender in Black Women's Biographies." *Gender & Society* 13: 120–137.

Burnstein, Paul, and Marie Bricher. 1997. "Problem Definition and Public Policy: Congressional Committees Confront Work, Family, and Gender, 1945–1990." *Social Forces* 75: 135–169.

Burr, Vivian. 2015. *Social Constructionism*, 3rd edition. New York: Routledge.

Calhoun, Craig. 1994. "Social Theory and the Politics of Identity." In *Social Theory and the Politics of Identity*, edited by Craig Calhoun, 9–36. Cambridge, MA: Blackwell.

Calhoun, Craig, and Jonathan VanAntwerpen. 2007. "Orthodoxy, Heterodoxy, and Hierarchy: 'Mainstream' Sociology and its Challengers." In *Sociology in America: A History*, edited by Craig Calhoun, 367–410. Chicago: University of Chicago Press.

Campbell, John L. 2002. "Ideas, Politics, and Public Policy." *Annual Review of Sociology* 28: 21–38.

Cancian, Francisca M. 1987. *Love in America: Gender and Self-Development*. Cambridge: Cambridge University Press.

Carnaghan, Ellen. 2016. "From Balcony to Barricade: Nationalism and Popular Mobilization in Georgia, Ukraine, and Russia." *Europe-Asia Studies* 68: 1579–1607.

Cerulo, Karen A. 1998. *Deciphering Violence: The Cognitive Structure of Right and Wrong*. New York: Routledge.

Chaitin, Julia. 2003. "Narratives and Story-Telling." *Beyond Intractability*. Guy Burgess and Heide Burgess (eds.) Conflict Information Consortium, University of Colorado, Boulder.

Chapman, Simon, Kim McLeod, Melanie Wakefield, and Simon Holding. 2005. "Impact of News of Celebrity Illness on Breast Cancer Screening: Kylie Minogue's Breast Cancer Diagnosis." *The Medical Journal of Australia* 183: 247–250.

Chavez, Leo. 2008. *The Latino Threat: Constructing Immigrants, Citizens, and the Nation*. Stanford, CA: Stanford University Press.

Clark, Candace. 1997. *Misery and Company: Sympathy in Everyday Life*. Chicago: University of Chicago Press.

Clark, Phillip G. 2007. "Understanding Aging and Disability Perspectives on Home Care: Uncovering Facts and Values in Public Policy Narratives and Discourse." *Canadian Journal on Aging* 26: 47–62.

Clawson, Rosalee A., and Rakuya Trice. 2000. "Poverty as We Know It: Media Portrayals of the Poor." *Public Opinion Quarterly* 64: 53–64.

Clément, Maéva, Thomas Lindemann, and Eric Sangar. 2017. "The 'Hero-Protector Narrative': Manufacturing Emotional Consent for the Use of Force." *Political Psychology* 38: 991–1008.

Clough, Patricia T. 2000. "Comments on Setting Criteria for Experimental Writing."*Qualitative Inquiry* 6: 278–291.

Cohen, Jodi R. 1997. "Poverty: Talk, Identity and Action." *Qualitative Inquiry* 3: 71–92.

Coles, Roberta L. 1998. "Peaceniks and Warmongers' Framing Fracas on the Home Front: Dominant and Opposition Discourse during the Persian Gulf Crisis." *The Sociological Quarterly* 39: 369–391.

Coles, Roberta L. 2002. "War and the Contest over National Identity." *The Sociological Review:* 28: 586–609.

Collins, Patricia Hill. 1989. "The Social Construction of Invisibility: Black Women's Poverty in Social Problems Discourse." In *Perspectives on Social Problems*, Volume 1, edited by James A. Holstein and Gale Miller, 77–94. Greenwich, CT: JAI Press.

Conley, J. M., and W. M. O'Barr. 1990. *Rules versus Relationships: The Ethnography of Legal Discourse*. Chicago: University of Chicago Press.

Copes, Heith, Andy Hochstetler, and Sveinung Sandberg. 2015. "Using a Narrative Framework to Understand the Drugs and Violence Nexus." *Criminal Justice Review* 40: 32–46.

Cramer, Katherine J. 2016. *The Politics of Resentment: Rural Consciousness in Wisconsin and the Rise of Scott Walker*. Chicago: University of Chicago Press.

Crotty, Michael. 2015. *The Foundations of Social Research: Meaning and Perspective in the Research Process*. Thousand Oaks, CA: Sage.

Cullen, Jim. 2003. *The American Dream: A Short History of an Idea that Shaped a Nation.* New York: Oxford University Press.

D'Andrade, Roy. 1995. *The Development of Cognitive Anthropology.* Cambridge: Cambridge University Press.

Davis, Joseph E. 2002. "Narrative and Social Movements: The Power of Stories." In *Stories of Change: Narrative and Social Movements*, edited by Joseph E. Davis, 3–30. Albany, NY: State University of New York Press.

Dearin, Ray D. 1997. "The American Dream as Depicted in Robert J. Dole's 1996 Presidential Nomination Acceptance Speech." *Presidential Studies Quarterly* 27: 698–713.

Deeb-Sossa, Natalia. 2007. "Helping the 'Neediest of the Needy': An Intersectional Analysis of Moral-Identity Construction at a Community Health Clinic." *Gender & Society* 21: 749–772.

deGoede, Marieke. 1996. "Ideology in the US Welfare Debate: Neo-Liberal Representations of Poverty." *Discourse & Society* 7: 317–357.

Denzin, Norman K., and Yvonna S. Lincoln. 2000. "Introduction: The Discipline and Practice of Qualitative Research." In *Handbook of Qualitative Research*, 2nd edition, edited by Norman K. Denzin and Yvonna S. Lincoln, 1–29. Thousand Oaks, CA: Sage.

Diaz, Lizbeth. 2018. "Crime Menaces Migrants on Mexico Border as Tijuana Declares Crisis." *Reuters News*, November 23. https://www.reuters.com/article/us-usa-immigration-caravan-kids/crime-menaces-migrants-on-mexico-border-as-tijuana-declares-crisis-idUSKCN1NT007.

DiMaggio, Paul. 1997. "Culture and Cognition." *Annual Review of Sociology* 23: 263–287.

Domesticshelters.org. 2018. "Survivor: Christopher Anderson: Severe neglect and abuse as a child sent one man on a lifetime journey of healing." https://www.domesticshelters.org/domestic-violence-articles-information/survivor-christopher-anderson.

Domesticshelters.org. 2018. "Running for her Life." https://www.domesticshelters.org/domestic-violence-articles-information/running-for-her-life.

Drash, Wayne. 2017. "Stopping the Opioid Crisis in the Womb." *CNN*, May 5. https://www.cnn.com/2017/05/05/health/opioid-detox-during-pregnancy/index.html.

Dreamer Stories: Portraits of American Dreamers. https://www.dreamerstories.com.

Du, Ying Roselyn. 2016. "Same Events, Different Stories: Internet Censorship in the Arab Spring Seen from China." *Journalism & Mass Communication Quarterly* 93: 99–117.

Duany, Jorge. 1998. "Reconstructing Racial Identity: Ethnicity, Color, and Class among Dominicans in the United States and Puerto Rico." *Latin American Perspectives* 25: 147–172.

Dubriwny, Tasha. 2009. "Constructing Breast Cancer in the News: Betty Ford and the Evolution of the Breast Cancer Patient." *Journal of Communication Inquiry* 33: 104–125.

Dunn, Jennifer L. 2001. "Innocence Lost: Accomplishing Victimization in Intimate Stalking Cases." *Symbolic Interaction* 24: 285–313.

Dunn, Jennifer. 2002. *Courting Disaster: Intimate Stalking, Culture, and Criminal Justice.* New York: Aldine deGruyter.

Durkheim, Emile. 1961. *The Elementary Forms of Religious Life.* New York: MacMillan.

Eakin, Paul John. 2007. "The Economy of Narrative Identity." *History of Political Economy* 39: 117–133.

Eberle, Thomas S. 2009. "Global Differences in Conceptualizing Culture: An Ongoing Colloquium." *Cultural Processes: Newsletter of the Research Network, Sociology of Culture, European Sociological Association* 1: 5–38.

Edelman, Murray. 1977. *Political Language: Words That Succeed and Policies That Fail.* New York: Academic Press.

Edgley, Charles, and Dennis Brissett. 1990. "Health Nazis and the Cult of the Perfect Body: Some Polemical Observations." *Symbolic Interaction* 13: 257–279.

Edwards, Jason A., and Richard Herder. 2012. "Melding a New Immigration Narrative? President George W. Bush and the Immigration Debate." *The Harvard Journal of Communication* 23: 40–65.

Emerson, Robert M. 1997. "Constructing Serious Violence and its Victims: Processing a Domestic Violence Restraining Order." In *Social Problems in Everyday Life: Studies of Social*

Problems Work, edited by Gale Miller and James A. Holstein, 191–218. Greenwich, CT: JAI Press.

Entman, Robert M. 2003. "Cascading Activation: Contesting the White House's Frame after 9/11." *Political Communication* 20: 415–432.

Etter-Lewis, Gwendolyn. 1991. "Standing Up and Speaking Out: African American Women's Narrative Legacy." *Discourse & Society* 2: 425–437.

Ewick, Patricia, and S. Silbey. 1995. "Subversive Stories and Hegemonic Tales: Toward a Sociology of Narrative." *Law and Society Review* 29: 197–226.

Express Tribune. "Latest Reports Suggest Actor May Have Been Making Her Ex-husband Brad Pitt Look Bad Deliberately," September 16. https://tribune.com.pk/story/1508107/angelina-jolie-real-villain-divorce-brad-pitt/.

Faux, Zeke. 2017. "Millions Are Hounded for Debt They Don't Owe. One Victim Fought Back, With a Vengeance." *Bloomberg News*, December 18. https://www.msn.com/en-us/news/us/millions-are-hounded-for-debt-they-don%E2%80%99t-owe-one-victim-fought-back-with-a-vengeance/ar-BBGIpzP?li=AA4ZnC&ocid=spartandhp.

Federation for American Immigration Reform. "Examples of Serious Crimes by Illegal Aliens." https://fairus.org/issue/illegal-immigration/examples-serious-crimes-illegal-aliens.

Feeding America. n.d. "Hunger in America." http://www.feedingamerica.org/hunger-in-america/hunger-stories/yourstories/?gclid=CNGggreemtMCFVhahgodqewMxQ.

Fernandez, Mike. 2018. "As Florida Governor, Andrew Gillum will Lead More of us Toward the American Dream." *Miami Herald*, October 10. https://www.miamiherald.com/opinion/op-ed/article219775210.html.

Ferrence, Matthew. 2012. "You Are and You Ain't: Story and Literature as Redneck Resistance." *Journal of Appalachian Studies* 18: 113–130.

Fine, Gary Alan. 2002. "The Storied Group: Social Movements as 'Bundles of Narratives.'" In *Stories of Change: Narrative and Social Movements*," edited by Joseph E. Davis, 229–246. Albany, NY: State University of New York Press.

Fischer, Frank. 2003. *Reframing Public Policy: Discursive Politics and Deliberative Practices*. New York: Oxford University Press.

Fisher, Walter R. 1973. "Reaffirmation and Subversion of the American Dream." *Quarterly Journal of Speech* 59: 160–167.

Fisher, Walter R. 1984. "Narration as a Human Communication Paradigm: The Case of Public Moral Argument." *Communication Monographs* 51: 1–22.

Folpp, Leti. 2002. "The Citizen and the Terrorist." *UCLA Law Review* 49: 1575–1600.

Fox, Kathryn J. 1999. "Changing Violent Minds: Discursive Correction and Resistance in the Cognitive Treatment of Violent Offenders in Prison." *Social Problems* 46: 88–103.

Frank, Arthur W. 1995. *The Wounded Storyteller: Body, Illness, and Ethics*. Chicago: University of Chicago Press.

Frank, Thomas. 2004. *What's the Matter with Kansas?* New York: Picador.

Frank, Lauren B., Sheila T. Murphy, Joyee S. Chatterjee, Meghan B. Moran, and Lourdes Baezconde-Garbanati. 2015. "Telling Stories, Saving Lives: Creating Narrative Health Messages." *Health Communication* 30: 154–163.

Friedland, Roger, and Robert Alford. 1991. "Bringing Society Back in: Symbols, Practices, and Institutional Contradictions." In *The New Institutionalism in Organizational Analysis*, edited by Walter W. Powell and Paul DiMaggio, 223–262. Chicago: University of Chicago Press.

Frye, Northrop. 1957. *Anatomy of Criticism*. New Jersey: Princeton University Press.

Furedi, Frank. 2004. *Therapy Culture: Cultivating Vulnerability in an Uncertain Age*. New York: Routledge.

Gaines, Brian J. 2002. "Where's the Rally: Approval and Trust of the President, Cabinet, and Congress since September 11." *Political Science & Politics* 35: 531–536.

Gamson, Joshua. 1998. *Freaks Talk Back: Tabloid Talk Shows and Sexual Nonconformity*. Chicago: University of Chicago Press.

Ganim, Sara. "Jerry Sandusky's 'Victim Four' tells his story of alleged abuse for years by Sandusky as a surrogate father." *The Patriot News*, November 17. http://www.pennlive.com/midstate/index.ssf/2011/11/jerry_sanduskys_victim_four_te.html.

Gans, Herbert J. 2012. "Against Culture versus Structure." *Identities: Global Studies in Culture and Power* 19: 125–135.

Garrard, Eve. 2002. "Evil as an Explanatory Concept." *The Monist* 85: 320–336.

Garrison, Spencer. 2018. "On the Limits of 'Trans Enough': Authenticating Trans Identity Narratives." *Gender & Society* 32: 613–637.

Gergen, Kenneth J. 1994. *Realities and Relationships: Soundings in Social Construction.* Cambridge, MA: Harvard University Press.

Gergen, Kenneth J., and Mary M. Gergen. 1983. "Narratives of the Self." In *Studies in Social Identity*, edited by Theodore R. Sarbin and Karl E. Scheibe, 254–273. New York: Praeger.

Gergen, Mary. 1994. "The Social Construction of Personal Histories: Gendered Lives in Popular Autobiographies." In *Constructing the Social*, edited by Theodore R. Sarbin and John I. Kitsuse, 19–44. Thousand Oaks, CA: Sage.

Gertz, Clifford. 1973. *The Interpretation of Cultures.* New York: Basic Books.

Gest, Justin. 2016. *The New Minority: White Working Class Politics in an Age of Immigration and Inequality.* New York: Oxford University Press.

Gordon, Linda. 1994. *Pitied But Not Entitled: Single Moms and the History of Welfare.* New York: Free Press.

Gordon, Steven L. 1990. "Social Structural Effects on Emotions." In *Research Agendas in the Sociology of Emotions*, edited by Theodore D. Kemper, 134–179. Albany, NY: State University of New York Press.

Graebner, William. 2002. "The End of Liberalism: Narrating Welfare's Decline, from the Moynihan Report (1965) to the Personal Responsibility and Work Opportunity Act (1996)." *The Journal of Policy History* 14: 170–190.

Griffin, Justine. 2018. "I'm Not Using These Drugs to Get High." *Tampa Bay Times*, February 11, 2018: A1.

Gring-Pemble, Lisa M. 2001. "'Are We Going to Now Govern by Anecdote?': Rhetorical Constructions of Welfare Recipients in Congressional Hearings, Debates, and Legislation, 1992–1996." *Quarterly Journal of Speech* 87: 341–365.

Griswold, Wendy. 1987. "A Methodological Framework for the Sociology of Culture." *Sociological Methodology* 17: 1–35.

Gubrium, Jaber, and James A. Holstein. 1997. *The New Language of Qualitative Method.* New York: Oxford University Press.

Gubrium, Jaber F., and James A. Holstein. 2002. *Handbook of Interview Research: Context and Method.* Thousand Oaks, CA: Sage.

Gubrium, Jaber F., and James A. Holstein. 2009. *Analyzing Narrative Reality.* Thousand Oaks, CA: Sage.

Guetzkow, Joshua. 2010. "Beyond Deservingness: Congressional Discourse on Poverty, 1964–1996." *Annals of the American Academy of Political and Social Science.* 629: 173–197.

Gusfield, Joseph. 1981. *The Culture of Pubic Problems: Drinking-Driving and the Symbolic Order.* Chicago: University of Chicago Press.

Hancock, Ange-Marie. 2004. *The Politics of Disgust: The Public Identity of the Welfare Queen.* New York: New York University Press.

Handler, Joel F., and Yeheskel Hasenfeld. 1991. *The Moral Construction of Poverty: Welfare Reform in America.* Thousand Oaks, CA: Sage.

Harré, Rom 1986. "An Outline of the Social Constructionist Viewpoint." In *The Social Construction of Emotions*, edited by Rom Harré, 2–13. New York: Basil Blackwell.

Harvey, Mary R., Elliot G. Mishler, Karestan Koenen, and Patricia A. Harney. 2000. "In the Aftermath of Sexual Abuse: Making and Remaking Meaning in Narratives of Trauma and Recovery." *Narrative Inquiry* 10: 291–311.

Heritage, John. 1984. *Garfinkel and Ethnomethodology.* New York: Polity Press.

Hewitt, Jonathan. 2012. "His Name Was Steven: A 13-Year-Old Victim of Bullycide." *Huffington Post*, October 16. https://www.huffingtonpost.com/jonathan-hewitt/bullying_b_1968592.html.

Hitlin, Steven and Stephen Vaisey. 2013. "The New Sociology of Morality." *Annual Review of Sociology* 39: 51–68.

Hochschild, Arlie Russell. 1979. "Emotion Work, Feeling Rules, and Social Structure." *American Journal of Sociology* 85: 551–575.

Hochschild, Arlie Russell. 2016. *Strangers in Their Own Land: Anger and Mourning in the American Right.* New York: New Press.

Hochschild, Jennifer L. 1995. *Facing up to the American Dream: Race, Class, and the Soul of the Nation.* New Jersey: Princeton University Press.

Hochschild, Jennifer L. 2001. "Public Schools and the American Dream." *Dissent* (fall): 35–38.

Hoffmaster, Barry. 2014. "From Applied Ethics to Narrative Ethics: The Rationality and Morality of Telling Stories in Bioethics." *Hastings Center Report*, May–June: 4–5.

Höijer, Birgitta. 2004. "The Discourse of Global Compassion: The Audience and Media Reporting of Human Suffering." *Media, Culture & Society* 26: 513–531.

Holstein, James A., and Gale Miller. 1990. "Rethinking Victimization: An Interactional Approach to Victimology." *Symbolic Interaction* 12: 102–122.

Holstein, James, and Jaber F. Gubrium. 2000. *The Self We Live By: Narrative Identity in a Postmodern* World. New York: Oxford University Press.

Holstein, James A., and Jaber F. Gubrium (eds). 2012. *Varieties of Narrative Analysis.* Thousand Oaks, CA: Sage.

Huddy, Leonie, Nadia Khatib, and Theresa Capelos. 2002. "The Polls-Trends: Reactions to the Terrorist Attacks of September 11, 2001." *Public Opinion Quarterly* 66: 418–430.

Huiberts, Eline, and Stijn Joye. 2018. "Close, but not Close Enough? Audience's Reactions to Domesticated Distant Suffering in International News Coverage." *Media, Culture, & Society* 40: 333–347.

Hutcheson, John, David Domke, Andre Billeaudeaux, and Philip Garland. 2004. "U.S. National Identity, Political Elites, and a Patriotic Press Following September 11." *Political Communication* 21: 27–50.

Irvine, Leslie. 1999. *Codependent Forevermore: The Invention of Self in a Twelve Step Group.* Chicago: University of Chicago Press.

Jackson, Brandon A. 2012. "Bonds of Brotherhood: Emotional and Social Support among College Black Men." *Annals of the American Association of Political and Social Science* 642: 61–71.

Jacobs, Keith, Jim Kemeny, and Tony Manzi. 2003. "Power, Discursive Space and Institutional Practices in the Construction of Housing Problems." *Housing Studies* 18: 429–446.

Jacobs, Ronald N., and Sarah Sobieraj. 2007. "Narrative and Legitimacy: U.S. Congressional Debates About the Nonprofit Sector." *Sociological Theory* 25: 1–25.

Jasper, James M. 1992. "The Politics of Abstractions: Instrumental and Moralist Rhetoric in Public Debate." *Social Research* 59: 315–344.

Jasper, James M. 1997. *The Art of Moral Protest: Culture, Biography, and Creativity in Social Movements.* Chicago: University of Chicago Press.

Jasper, James M., Michael Young, Elke Zuern. 2018. "Character Work in Social Movements." *Theoretical Sociology* 47: 113–131.

Jeffries, Julian. 2009. "Do Undocumented Students Play by the Rules? Meritocracy in the Media." *Critical Inquiry in Language Studies* 6: 15–38.

Jimenez, Jesus. 2017. "An Immigrant's Take on Today's American Dream." *Sucess.com*, June 8. https://www.success.com/blog/an-immigrants-take-on-todays-american-dream.

Johnson, Caitlin. 2017. "New Bus Routes Strand Many." *Tampa Bay Times*, October 7: A1.

Johnson, Richard. 2002. "Defending Ways of Life: The (Anti-)Terrorist Rhetorics of Bush and Blair." *Theory, Culture & Society* 19: 211–31.

Kane, Anne. 2000. "Reconstructing Culture in Historical Explanation: Narratives as Cultural Structure and Practice." *History & Theory* 39: 311–330.

Keen, Ian. 2015. "The Language of Morality." *The Australian Journal of Anthropology* 26: 332–344.

Kennley, Ivy. 1999. "That Single-Mother Element: How White Employers Typify Black Women." *Gender & Society* 13: 168–192.

Kinderman, Robin. 2016. "A Welfare Story." *The New American* https://www.thenewamerican.com/culture/item/24193-a-welfare-story.

Kirkman, Maggie. 2002. "What's the Plot? Applying Narrative Theory to Research in Psychology." *Australian Psychologist* 37: 30–38.

Kirkman, Maggie, Lyn Harrison, Lynne Hillier, and Priscilla Pyett. 2001. "'I Know I'm Doing a Good Job': Canonical and Autobiographical Narratives of Teenage Mothers." *Culture, Health & Sexuality* 3: 279–294.

Klapp, Orin. 1954. "Heroes, Villains, and Fools as Agents of Social Control." *American Sociological Review* 19: 56–62.

Koh, Michael, ed. 2013. "41 Short Stories Of Unforgettable Evil From 41 People." http://thoughtcatalog.com/michael-koh/2013/09/41-short-stories-of-unforgettable-evil-from-41-people/.

Kohli, Sonali, and Santa Cruz, Nicole. 2018. "California shooting victim was devoted to helping his fellow vets." *Los Angeles Times*, November 10. https://www.msn.com/en-us/news/us/california-shooting-victim-was-devoted-to-helping-his-fellow-vets/ar-BBPxZ4m?ocid=spartandhp.

Kroll-Smith, Steve. 2000. "The Social Production of the 'Drowsy Person.'" In *Perspectives on Social Problems*, Volume 12, edited by James A. Holstein and Gale Miller, 89–109. Greenwich, CT: JAI Press.

Kusow, Abdi M., and Mohamed A. Eno. 2015. "Formula Narratives and the Making of Social Stratification and Inequality." *Sociology of Race and Ethnicity* 1: 409–423.

Lakoff, George. 1996. *Moral Politics: What Conservatives Know that Liberals Don't.* Chicago: University of Chicago Press.

Lakoff, George. 2004. *Don't Think of An Elephant: Know Your Values and Frame the Debate.* White River Junction, VT: Chelsea Green Publishing.

Lakoff, George. 2009. *The Political Mind: A Cognitive Scientist's Guide to your Brain and its Politics.* New York: Penguin Books.

Lamb, Sharon. 1999. "Constructing the Victim: Popular Images and Lasting Labels." In *New Versions of Victims: Feminists Struggle with the Concept*, edited by Sharon Lamb, 108–138. New York: New York University Press.

Lambek, Michael, and Jacqueline S. Solway. 2001. "Just Anger: Scenarios of Indignation in Botswana and Madagascar." *Ethnos* 77: 49–72.

Lamont, Michèle. 2000a. *The Dignity of Working Men: Morality and the Boundaries of Race, Class, and Immigration.* New York: Russell Sage Foundation.

Lamont, Michèle. 2000b. "Meaning-Making in Cultural Sociology: Broadening Our Agenda." *Contemporary Sociology* 129: 602–607.

Lamont, Michèle, and Marcel Fournier. 1992. "Introduction." In *Cultivating Differences: Symbolic Boundaries and the Making of Inequality*, edited by Michèle Lamont and Marcel Fournier, 1–20. Chicago: University of Chicago Press.

Lamont, Michèle, and Virág Molnár. 2002. "The Study of Boundaries in the Social Sciences." *Annual Review of Sociology* 28: 167–195.

Lamont, Michèle, and Mario Luis Small. 2008. "How Culture Matters: Enriching Our Understanding of Poverty." In *The Colors of Poverty: Why Racial and Ethnic Disparities Persist*, edited by Ann Chih Lin and David R. Harris, 76–102. New York: Russell Sage Foundation.

Lamonth, Joe. July 4, 2011. "10 People Living the American Dream." *The Street.* https://www.thestreet.com/story/11173382/9/10-people-living-the-american-dream.html.

Lauby, Fanny. 2016. "Leaving the 'Perfect DREAMer' Behind? Narratives and Mobilization in Immigration Reform." *Social Movement Studies* 15: 374–387.

Lehrner, Amy, and Nicole E. Allen. 2008. "Social Change Movements and the Struggle Over Meaning-Making: A Case Study of Domestic Violence Narratives." *American Journal of Community Psychology* 42: 220–234.

Lemert, Edwin M. 1997. *The Trouble With Evil: Social Control at the Edge of Morality.* Albany, NY: State University of New York Press.

Lifton, Robert. 1973. *Home from the War: Learning from Vietnam Veterans.* Boston: Beacon.

Linde, Charlotte. 1993. *Life Stories: The Creation of Coherence.* New York: Oxford University Press.

Linde, Charlotte. 2009. *Working the Past: Narrative and Institutional Memory.* New York: Oxford University Press.

Linde, Charlotte. 2010. "Social Issues in the Understanding of Narrative." Papers from the Association for the Advancement of Artificial Intelligence, Fall symposium. Association for the Advancement of Artificial Intelligence.

Lipsky, Michael. 1980. *Street-Level Bureaucracy: Dilemmas of the Individual in Public Services*. New York: Russell Sage Foundation.

Loseke, Donileen R. 1992. *The Battered Woman and Shelters: The Social Construction of Wife Abuse*. Albany, NY: State University of New York Press.

Loseke, Donileen R. 2001. "Lived Realities and Formula Stories of 'Battered Women.'" In *Institutional Selves: Troubled Identities in a Postmodern World*, edited by James A. Holstein and Jaber Gubrium, 107–126. New York: Oxford University Press.

Loseke, Donileen R. 2003. *Thinking About Social Problems: An Introduction to Constructionist Perspectives*, 2nd edition. Piscataway, NJ: Transaction.

Loseke, Donileen R. 2007. "The Study of Identity as Cultural, Institutional, Organizational, and Personal Narratives: Theoretical and Empirical Integrations." *The Sociological Quarterly* 48: 661–688.

Loseke, Donileen R. 2009. "Examining Emotion as Discourse: Emotion Codes and Presidential Speeches Justifying War." *The Sociological Quarterly* 50: 499–526.

Loseke, Donileen R. 2012. "The Empirical Analysis of Formula Stories." In *Varieties of Narrative Analysis*, edited by James A. Holstein and Jaber F. Gubrium, 251–272. Thousand Oaks, CA: Sage.

Loseke, Donileen R., and Kirsten Fawcett. 1995. "Appealing Appeals: Constructing Moral Worthiness, 1912–1917." *The Sociological Quarterly* 36: 61–78.

Loseke, Donileen R., and Margarethe Kusenbach. 2008. "The Social Construction of Emotion." In *Handbook of Constructionist Research*, edited by James A. Holstein and Jaber F. Gubrium, 511–530. New York: Guilford Press.

Lowney, Kathleen S. 1999. *Baring Our Souls: TV Talk Shows and the Religion of Recovery*. New York: Aldine deGruyter.

Lutz, Catherine. 1986. "Emotion, Thought, and Estrangement: Emotion as a Cultural Category." *Cultural Anthropology* 1: 287–309.

Lyons, Peter, and Barbara Rittner. 1998. "The Construction of the Crack Babies Phenomenon as a Social Problem." *American Journal of Orthopsychiatry* 68: 303–320.

MacIntyre, Alistar. 1984. *After Virtue: A Study in Moral Theory*. Notre Dame, IN: University of Notre Dame Press.

Maines, David R. 1991. "The Storied Nature of Health and Diabetic Self-Help Groups." In *Advances in Medical Sociology*, Volume 2, edited by Gary L. Albrecht and Judith A. Levy, 185–202. Greenwich, CT: JAI.

Marcus, George E. 2000. "Emotions in Politics." *Annual Review of Political Science* 3: 221–250.

Marcus, George E. 2002. *The Sentimental Citizen: Emotion in Democratic Politics*. University Park, PA: The Pennsylvania State University Press.

Marvasti, Amir B. 2002. "Constructing the Service-Worthy Homeless Through Narrative Editing." *Journal of Contemporary Ethnography* 31: 615–651.

Mason-Schrock, Douglas. 1996. "Transsexuals' Narrative Construction of the 'True Self.'" *Social Psychology Quarterly* 59: 176–192.

Mayberry, Maralee. 2006. "Identity work and LGBT Youth: The Story of Salt Lake City Gay-Straight Alliance." *Journal of Gay & Lesbian Issues in Education* 4: 13–32.

Mayer, Frederick W. 2014. *Narrative Politics: Stories and Collective Action*. New York: Oxford University Press.

Mazzeo, Christopher, Sara Rab, and Susan Eachus. 2003. "Work-First or Work-Only: Welfare Reform, State Policy, and Access to Postsecondary Education." *Annuals of the American Academy of Political and Social Sciences* 586: 144–171.

McAdams, Dan P. 1996. "Personality, Modernity, and the Storied Self: A Contemporary Framework for Studying Persons." *Psychological Inquiry* 7: 295–293.

McCarthy, E. Doyle. 1989. "Emotions are Social Things: An Essay in the Sociology of Emotions." In *The Sociology of Emotions: Original Essays and Research Reports*, Volume 9, edited by David D. Franks and E. Doyle McCarthy, 51–72. Greenwich, CT: JAI Press.

McCarthy. E. Doyle. 2017. *Emotional Lives: Dramas of Identity in an Age of Mass Media.* Cambridge, MA: Cambridge University Press.

McGinnis, Theresa A. 2009. "Seeing Possible Futures: Khmer Youth and the Discourse of the American Dream." *Anthropology & Education Quarterly* 40: 62–81.

McHugh, Katie. 2016. "Remembering Grant Ronnebeck: A Victim of a Mexican Cartel and Illegal Alien Crime." *Breitbart News*, June 10. http://www.breitbart.com/big-government/2016/06/10/remembering-grant-ronnebeck-a-victim-of-a-mexican-cartel-and-illegal-alien-crime/.

McIntosh, James, and Neil McKeganey. 2000. "Addicts' Narratives of Recovery from Drug Use: Constructing a Non-Addict Identity." *Social Science & Medicine* 50: 1501–1510.

McKendy, John P. 1992. "Ideological Practices and the Management of Emotions: The Case of 'Wife Abusers.'" *Critical Sociology* 19: 61–80.

McQueen, Amy, Matthew W. Kreuter, Bindu Kalesan, and Kassandra I. Alcaraz. 2011. "Understanding Narrative Effects: The Impact of Breast Cancer Survivor Stories on Message Processing, Attitudes, and Beliefs Among African American Women." *Health Psychology* 30: 674–682.

Medhurst, Martin J. 2016. "LBJ, Reagan, and the American Dream: Competing Visions of Liberty." *Presidential Studies Quarterly* 46: 98–124.

Merskin, Debra. 2004. "The Construction of Arabs as Enemies: Post September 11 Discourse of George W. Bush." *Mass Communication and Society* 7: 157–175.

Metcalfe, D., C. Price, J. Powell. 2010. "Media Coverage and Public Reaction to a Celebrity Cancer Diagnosis." *Journal of Public Health* 33: 80–85.

Mildorf, Jarmila. 2002. "'Opening Up a Can of Worms': Physicians' Narrative Construction of Knowledge about Domestic Violence." *Narrative Inquiry* 12: 233–260.

Milkman, Ruth. 2014. "Millennial Movements: Occupy Wall Street and the Dreamers." *Dissent* 61: 55–59.

Miller, Gale. 1991. *Enforcing the Work Ethic: Rhetoric and Everyday Life in a Work Incentive Program.* Albany, NY: State University of New York Press.

Miller, Gale, and James A. Holstein. 1989. "On the Sociology of Social Problems." In *Perspectives on Social Problems*, Volume 1, edited by James A. Holstein and Gale Miller, 1–18. Greenwich, CT: JAI Press.

Mishler, Elliot G. 1995. "Models of Narrative Analysis: A Typology." *Journal of Narrative and Life History* 5: 87–123.

Moerk, Ernst L., and Faith Pincus. 2000. "How to Make Wars Acceptable." *Peace & Change* 25: 1–22.

Moses, Jonathon W., and Torbjørn L. Knutsen. 2012. *Ways of Knowing: Competing Methodologies in Social and Political Research*, 2nd edition. New York: Palgrave McMillan.

Moïsi, Dominique. 2009. *The Geopolitics of Emotion: How Cultures of Fear, Humiliation, and Hope are Reshaping the World.* New York: Anchor Books.

Mothers Against Drunk Driving. 2017. "Officer Brent Wisdom." *MADD.org*, September 1. https://www.madd.org/blog/officer-brent-wisdom/.

Murphy, John M. 2003. "Our Mission and Our Moment: George W. Bush and September 11th." *Rhetoric & Public Affairs* 6: 607–632.

Nabi, Robin L., and Melanie C. Green. 2015. "The Role of a Narrative's Emotional Flow in Promoting Persuasive Outcomes." *Media Psychology* 18: 137–162.

Neubeck, Kenneth J., and Noel A. Cazenave. 2001. *Welfare Racism: Playing the Race Card Against America's Poor.* New York: Routledge.

Neville-Shepard, Ryan. 2017. "Constrained by Duality: Third-Party Master Narratives in the 2016 Presidential Election." *American Behavioral Scientist* 61: 414–427.

Nicholls, Walter J., and Tara Fiorito. 2015. "Dreamers Unbound: Immigrant Youth Mobilizing." *New Labor Forum* 24: 86–92.

Nolan, Hamilton. 2012. "Hello from the Underclass: Unemployment Stories." *The Gawker*, Volume 1, July 19. http://gawker.com/5927342/hello-from-the-underclass-unemployment-stories-vol-one.

Nolan, James L. Jr. 2002. "Drug Court Stories: Transforming American Jurisprudence." In *Stories of Change: Narrative and Social Movements*, edited by Joseph E. Davis, 149–178. Albany, NY: State University of New York Press.

Nunberg, Geoffrey. 2004. *Going Nucular: Language, Politics, and Culture in Confrontational Times.* New York: Public Affairs.

Nunberg, Geoffrey. 2006. *Talking Right: How Conservatives Turned Liberalism into a Tax-Raising, Latte-Drinking, Sushi-Eating, Volvo-Driving, New York Times-Reading, Body-Piercing, Hollywood-Loving, Left Wing Freak Show.* New York: Public Affairs.

O'Connor, Brendon. 2001. "The Protagonists and Ideas Behind the Personal Responsibility and Work Opportunity Reconciliation Act of 1996: The Enactment of a Conservative Welfare System." *Social Justice* 28: 4–32.

Obama, Barack. 2004. "Reclaiming the Promise to the People." Keynote Address, Democratic National Convention, Boston, Massachusetts. July 27, 2004.

Obama, Barack. 2006. "Comments to Graduating Class." Northwestern University, June 19. https://www.northwestern.edu/newscenter/stories/2006/06/barack.html.

Olive, Andrea, Vagisha Gunasekava, and Leigh Raymond. 2012. "Normative Beliefs in State Policy Choice." *Political Research Quarterly* 65: 642–655.

Ong, Jonathan Corpus. 2014. "'Witnessing' or 'Mediating' Distant Suffering? Ethical Questions across Moments of Text, Production, and Reception." *Television & New Media* 15: 179–196.

Oprah's Lifeclass. 2013. "Bishop T.D. Jakes Gives Feuding Sisters A Reality Check." *OWN* network, September 27. http://www.huffingtonpost.com/2013/09/27/td-jakes-oprahs-life-class_n_3991679.html.

Ortiz, Gabe. "Undocumented dad may be deported before he can watch his daughter graduate from medical school." *Daily Kos*, March 27. https://www.dailykos.com/stories/2018/03/27/1752487/-Undocumented-dad-may-be-deported-before-he-can-watch-his-daughter-gradu-ate-from-medical-school.

Padamsee, Tasleem J. 2009. Culture in Connection: Re-contextualizing Ideational Processes in the Analysis of Policy Development." *Social Politics* 16: 413–445.

Patterson, Orlando 2014. "Making Sense of Culture." *Annual Review of Sociology* 40: 1–30.

Pemberton, Antony, Pauline G. M. Aarten, and Eva Mulder. 2018. "Stories as Property: Narrative Ownership as a Key Concept in Victims' Experiences with Criminal Justice." *Criminology & Criminal Justice*, 1–17.

Persall, Steve. 2017. "Oscar Winner Viola Davis Tells USF Crowd: 'Own Your Own Story." *Tampa Bay Times*, April 4. https://www.tampabay.com/news/humaninterest/oscar-winner-viola-davis-tells-usf-crowd-own-your-own-story.

Petonito, Gina. 1992. "'Constructing Americans': 'Becoming American,' 'Loyalty,' and Japanese Internment During World War II." In *Perspectives on Social Problems*, Volume 4, edited by James A. Holstein and Gale Miller, 93–107. Greenwich, CT: JAI Press.

Pfau-Effinger, Birgit. 2005. "Culture and Welfare State Policies: Reflections on a Complex Interrelation." *International Journal of Social Policy* 34: 3–20.

Picart, Caroline Joan (Kay) S. 2003. "Rhetorically Reconfiguring Victimhood and Agency: The Violence Against Women Act's Civil Rights Clause." *Rhetoric & Public Affairs* 6: 97–126.

Pizarro, David. 2000. "Nothing More than Feelings? The Role of Emotions in Moral Judgment." *Journal for the Theory of Social Behaviour* 30: 355–375.

Plummer, Ken. 1995. *Telling Sexual Stories: Power, Change and Social Worlds.* New York: Routledge.

Polkinghorne, Donald E. 1991. "Narrative and Self-Concept." *Journal of Narrative and Life History* 1: 135–153.

Polletta, Francesca. 1997. "Culture and its Discontents: Recent Theorizing on the Cultural Dimensions of Protest." *Sociological Inquiry* 67: 431–50.

Polletta, Francesca. 2006. *It Was Like a Fever: Storytelling in Protest and Politics.* Chicago: University of Chicago Press.

Polletta, Francesca, Pang Ching Bobby Chen, Beth Gharrity Gardner, and Alice Motes. 2011. "The Sociology of Storytelling." *Annual Review of Sociology* 37: 109–130.

Pope, James. 2017. "Constructing the Refugee as Villain: An Analysis of Syrian Refugee Policy Narratives Used to Justify a State of Exception." *World Affairs*, Fall: 53–71.

Porter, Gayle. 2010. "Work Ethic and Ethical Work: Distortions in the American Dream." *Journal of Business Ethics* 96: 535–550.

Powell, Rachel. 2011. "Frames and Narratives as Tools for Recruiting and Sustaining Group Members: The Soulforce Equality Ride as a Social Movement Organization." *Sociological Inquiry* 81: 454–476.

Quadagno, Jill. 1994. *The Color of Welfare: How Racism Undermined the War on Poverty.* New York: Oxford University Press.

Quinlivan, Kathleen. 2002. "Whose Problem Is This? Queering the Framing of Lesbian and Gay Secondary School Students Within 'At Risk 'Discourses." *Journal of Gay & Lesbian Social Services* 14: 17–31.

Quinn, Naomi. 2005. "How to Reconstruct Schemas People Share, From What They Say." In *Finding Culture in Talk: A Collection of Methods,* edited by Naomi Quinn, 35–82. New York: Palgrave McMillan.

Rankin, Lindsay E., and Alice H. Eagly. 2008. "Is His Heroism Hailed and Hers Hidden? Women, Men, and the Social Construction of Heroism." *Psychology of Women Quarterly* 32: 414–422.

Rasmusen, Dani. n.d. "Caring." *Pass-it-on.com.* https://www.passiton.com/your-everyday-heroes/5278-dani-rasmussen.

Rawls, Anne Warfield. 2018. "The Wartime Narrative in US Sociology, 1940–1947: Stigmatizing Qualitative Sociology in the Name of 'Science.'" *European Journal of Social Theory* 2: 526–546.

Reich, Robert B. 2005. "Story Time: The Lost Art of Democratic Narrative." *The New Republic* March 28 and April 4: 16–19.

Riessman, Catherine K. 1989. "From Victim to Survivor: A Woman's Narrative Reconstruction of Marital Sexual Abuse." *Smith College Studies in Social Work* 59: 232–251.

Riessman, Catherine. 1992. "Making Sense of Marital Violence: One Woman's Narrative." In *Storied Lives: The Cultural Politics of Self-Understanding,* edited by George C. Rosenwald and Richard L. Ochberg, 231–249. New Haven, CT: Yale University Press.

Rochefort, David, and Roger Cobb. 1994. "Problem Definition: An Emerging Perspective." In *The Politics of Problem Definition: Shaping the Policy Agenda,* edited by David A. Rochefort and Roger W. Cobb, 1–31. Lawrence, KS: University of Kansas Press.

Roe, Emery. 1994. *Narrative Policy Analysis: Theory and Practice.* Durham, NC: Duke University Press.

Rossol, Josh. 2001. "The Medicalization of Deviance as an Interactive Achievement: The Construction of Compulsive Gambling." *Symbolic Interaction* 24: 315–341.

Rothenberg, Bess. 2002. "Movement Advocates as Battered Women's Storytellers: From Varied Experiences, One Message." In *Stories of Change: Narrative and Social Movements,* edited by Joseph E. Davis, 203–228. Albany, NY: State University of New York Press.

Rothenberg, Bess. 2003. "'We Don't Have Time for Social Change': Cultural Compromise and the Battered Women Syndrome." *Gender & Society* 17: 771–787.

Rowland, Robert C., and John M. Jones. 2007. "Recasting the American Dream and American Politics: Barack Obama's Keynote Address to the 2004 Democratic National Convention." *Quarterly Journal of Speech* 93: 425–448.

Roy, Kevin M. 2006. "Father Stories: A Life Course Examination of Paternal Identity Among Low-Income African American Men." *Journal of Family Issues* 27: 31–54.

Ruiz-Junco, Natalia. 2017. "Advancing the Sociology of Empathy: A Proposal." *Symbolic Interaction* 40: 414–435.

Samuel, Lawrence R. 2012. *The American Dream: A Cultural History.* New York: Syracuse University Press.

Samuels, Robert. 2017. "Kids' Health Insurance Hangs in the Balance and Parents Wonder What's Wrong With Congress." *Washington Post,* December 22. https://www.washingtonpost.com/politics/kids-health-insurance-hangs-in-balance-and-parents-wonder-whats-wrong-with-congress/2017/12/20/56792024-df5f-11e7-89e8-edec16379010_story.html?utm_term=.3c54eac29a6b.

Santiago-Irizarry, Vilma. 2001. *Medicalizing Ethnicity: The Construction of Latino Identity in a Psychiatric Setting.* Ithaca, NY: Cornell University Press.

Sanwicki, Patricia. n.d. "Why, Thank You," in "These Kids Said WHAT?! 29 Hilarious Real-Life Teacher Stories." *Reader's Digest* Editors http://www.rd.com/?s=why+thank+you.

Schneider, Anne, and Helen Ingram. 1993. "Social Construction of Target Populations: Implications for Politics and Policy." *American Political Science Review* 87: 334–347.

Schneider, Anne, and Mara Sidney. 2009. "What is Next for Policy Design and Social Construction Theory?" *The Policy Studies Journal* 37: 103–119.

Schneider, Joseph W. 1984. "Morality, Social Problems, and Everyday Life." In *Studies in the Sociology of Social Problems*, edited by Joseph W. Schneider and John I. Kitsuse, 180–206. Norwood, NJ: Ablex Publishing.

Schubert, James N., Patrick A. Stewart, and Margaret Ann Curran. 2002. "A Defining Presidential Movement: 9/11 and the Rally Effect." *Political Psychology* 23: 559–583.

Schudson, Michael. 1989. "How Culture Works." *Theory and Society* 18: 153–180.

Schuller, Regina A., and Neil Vidmar. 1992. "Battered Woman Syndrome as Evidence in the Courtroom: A Review of the Literature." *Law and Human Behavior* 16: 273–291.

Schutz, Alfred. 1970. *On Phenomenology and Social Relations.* Chicago, IL: University of Chicago Press.

Schwartz, Norbert 2000. "Emotion, Cognition, and Decision Making." *Cognition and Emotion* 14: 433–440.

Seccombe, Karen, Delores James, and Kimberly Battle Walters. 1998. "'They Think You Ain't Much of Nothing': The Social Construction of the Welfare Mother." *Journal of Marriage and the Family* 60: 849–865.

Selseng, Lillian Bruland. 2017. "Formula Stories of the 'Substance-Using Client': Addicted, Unreliable, Deteriorating, and Stigmatized." *Contemporary Drug Problems* 44: 87–104.

Sherman, Jennifer. 2009. *Those who Work, Those who Don't: Poverty, Morality, and Family in Rural America.* Minneapolis: University of Minnesota.

Shott, Susan. 1979. "Emotion and Social Life: A Symbolic Interactionist Agenda."*American Journal of Sociology* 84: 1317–1334.

Shuman, Amy. 2005. *Other People's Stories: Entitlement Claims and the Critique of Empathy.* Urbana, IL: University of Illinois Press.

Shuman, Amy, and Carol Bohmer (2004). "Representing Trauma: Political Asylum Narrative." *Journal of American Folklore* 117: 394–414.

Silva, Jennifer M. 2013. *Coming Up Short: Working-Class Adulthood in an Age of Uncertainty.* New York: Oxford University Press.

Simic, Charles. 2003. "Conspiracy of Silence." *New York Review of Books* February 27, 8–10.

Singer, Ben. 2001. *Melodrama and Modernity: Early Sensational Cinema and its Contexts.* New York: Columbia University Press.

Singer, Jefferson A. 2004. "Narrative Identity and Meaning Making Across the Adult Lifespan: An Introduction." *Journal of Personality* 72: 437–460.

Skocpol, Theda. 1995. *Social Policy in the United States: Future Possibilities in Historical Perspective.* Princeton: Princeton University Press.

Slovic, Paul. 2007. "'If I Look at the Mass I Will Never Act': Psychic Numbing and Genocide." *Judgment and Decision Making* 2: 79–95.

Small, Deborah A., George Loewenstein, and Paul Slovic. 2006. "Sympathy and Callousness: The Impact of Deliberative Thought on Donations to Identifiable and Statistical Victims." *Organizational Behavior and Human Decision Processes* 102: 143–153.

Smith, Curtis and Leon Anderson. 2018. "Fitting Stories: Outreach Worker Strategies for Housing Homeless Clients." *Journal of Contemporary Ethnography* 47: 535–550.

Smith, Philip. 2005. *Why War? The Cultural Logic of Iraq, the Gulf War, and Suez.* Chicago: University of Chicago Press.

Squire, Corinne. 2002. "White Trash Pride and the Exemplary Black Citizen: Counter-narratives of Gender, 'Race' and the Trailer Park in Contemporary Daytime Television Talk Shows." *Narrative Inquiry* 12: 155–172.

Starr, Paul. 1992. "Social Categories and Claims in the Liberal State." *Social Research* 59: 263–295.

Stearns, Peter N. 1990. "The Rise of Sibling Jealousy in the Twentieth Century." *Symbolic Interaction* 13: 83–101.

Stein, Arlene. 2009. "'As Far as They Knew I Came from France': Stigma, Passing, and Not Speaking about the Holocaust." *Symbolic Interaction* 32: 44–60.

Stein, Sandra J. 2001. "'These are your Title 1 Students': Policy Language in Educational Practice." *Policy Scienc*es 34: 135–56.

Steinmetz, George. 2005. "Introduction: Positivism and its Others in the Social Sciences." In *The Politics of Method in the Human Sciences: Positivism and its Epistemological Others*, edited by George Steinmetz, 1–58. Durham, NC: Duke University.

Stearns, Peter, and Carol Z. Stearns. 1985. "Emotionology: Clarifying the History of Emotions and Emotional Standards." *American Historical Review* 90: 13–836.

Stevens, Eric C. n.d. "Hero to Villain and Back Again: The Chris Herren story." *BreakingMuscle.com.* https://breakingmuscle.com/learn/hero-to-villain-and-back-again-the-chris-herren-story.

Stone, Deborah. 1989. "Causal Stories and the Formation of Policy Agendas." *Political Science Quarterly* 104: 281–300.

Stone, Deborah. 1997. *Policy Paradox: The Art of Political Decision Making*. New York: W.W. Norton.

Stroumboulopoulos, George. 2012. "The Price of Poverty: Young Boys in India Fish Coins Out of Rivers So Their Families Can Afford Food." http://www.cbc.ca/strombo/news/the-price-of-poverty-young-boys-in-india-fish-coins-out-of-river-so-their-f.".

Stryker, Robin, and Pamela Wald 2009. "Redefining Compassion to Reform Welfare: How Supporters of 1990s US Federal Welfare Reform Aimed for the Moral High Ground." *Social Politics* 16: 519–557.

Suarez Sang, Lucia I. 2018. "Tijuana Declares Humanitarian Crisis as Migrant Group That Split from Caravan Pushes Toward Border." *Fox News*, November 23. https://www.foxnews.com/world/tijuana-declares-humanitarian-crisis-as-small-migrant-group-pushes-toward-border.

Swidler, Ann. 1986. "Culture in Action: Symbols and Strategies." *American Sociological Review*, 273–286.

Swidler, Ann. 1995. "Cultural Power and Social Movements." In *Social Movements and Culture*, edited by Hank Johnston and Bert Kandermans, 25–40. Minneapolis: University of Minnesota Press.

Swidler, Ann. 2001. *Talk of Love: How Culture Matters*. Chicago: University of Chicago Press.

Szalavitz, Maia. 2018. "What the Media Gets Wrong About Opioids." *Columbia Journalism Review*, August 15. https://www.cjr.org/covering_the_health_care_fight/what-the-media-gets-wrong-about-opioids.php.

Tampa Bay Times, 2016. "Millions of Foreign Workers Face an Uncertain Future." June 26, 2016: 13A.

Toner, Kathleen. "Making Life Easier for Disabled Veterans." *CNN*, October 16. http://www.cnn.com/2013/02/14/us/cnnheroes-beatty-veterans-homes/index.html.

Townsend, Joseph. 1786 (1971). *A Dissertation on the Poor Laws by a Well-Wisher to Mankind*. Berkeley, CA: University of California Press.

United States House of Representatives. July 31, 1996. *Conference Report on H.R. 3734, Personal Responsibility and Work Opportunity Reconciliation Act of 1996*. H9392–H9424.

United We Dream. n.d. "Undocumented and Unafraid: Anthony's Story." https://unitedwedream.org/dreamer-narratives/blog-citizen-of-the-world/.

Vance, J. D. 2016. *Hillbilly Elegy: A Memoir of Family and Culture in Crisis*. New York: Harper.

Wagner-Pacifici, Robin Erica. 1986. *The Moro Morality Play: Terrorism as Social Drama*. Chicago, University of Chicago Press.

Weeks, Jeffrey. 1998. "The Sexual Citizen." *Theory, Culture & Society* 5: 35–52.

Weinberg, Darin. 2008. "The Philosophical Foundations of Constructionist Research." In *Handbook of Constructionist Research*, edited by James A. Holstein and Jaber F. Gubrium, 13–40. New York: Guilford Press.

Westin, Drew. 2007. *The Political Brain: The Role of Emotion in Deciding the Fate of the Nation*. New York: PublicAffairs.

Whippman, Ruth. August 11, 2016. "Why the American Dream is Making You Unhappy." *Time Magazine*. http://time.com/4446915/american-dream-making-you-unhappy/.

White, Hayden. 1980. "The Value of Narrativity in the Representation of Reality." *Critical Inquiry* 7: 5–27.

Wilburs, Loren E. 2016. *The Experience of Chronic Pain Management: A Multi-Voiced Narrative Analysis*. PhD Dissertation, Department of Sociology, University of South Florida.

Wilson, Drew. August 10, 2018. "Ross Spano Vows to Protect the American Dream in First CD-15 Ad." http://floridapolitics.com/archives/271479-ross-spano-vows-to-protect-american-dream-in-first-cd-15-ad.

Wood, Linda, and Heather Rennie. 1994. "Formulating Rape: The Discursive Construction of Victims and Villains." *Discourse and Society* 5: 125–148.

Zebregs, Simon, Bas van den Putte, Peter Neijens, and Anneke de Graaf. 2015. "The Differential Impact of Statistical and Narrative Evidence on Beliefs, Attitude, and Intention: A Meta-Analysis." *Health Communication* 30: 282–289.

Zerubavel, Eviatar. 1996. "Lumping and Splitting: Notes on Social Classification." *Sociological Forum* 11: 421–430.

Index

About the Author

Donileen R. Loseke is a professor of sociology at the University of South Florida. She has served as president of the Society for the Study of Symbolic Interaction and the Society for the Study of Social Problems. She is a former editor of the *Journal of Contemporary Ethnography* and a current editorial board member for *Social Psychology Quarterly* and *Symbolic Interaction*.

www.ingramcontent.com/pod-product-compliance
Lightning Source LLC
Chambersburg PA
CBHW022327280326
41932CB00010B/1250

* 9 7 8 1 4 9 8 5 7 7 7 9 3 *